Natural Language Engineering: Methods, Tasks and Applications

Natural Language Engineering: Methods, Tasks and Applications

Editors

Massimo Esposito
Giovanni Luca Masala
Aniello Minutolo
Marco Pota

MDPI • Basel • Beijing • Wuhan • Barcelona • Belgrade • Manchester • Tokyo • Cluj • Tianjin

Editors

Massimo Esposito
Institute for High Performance Computing and Networking
National Research Council of Italy
Naples
Italy

Giovanni Luca Masala
Institute for High Performance Computing and Networking
National Research Council of Italy
Naples
Italy

Aniello Minutolo
School of Computing
University of Kent
Canterbury
United Kingdom

Marco Pota
Institute for High Performance Computing and Networking
National Research Council of Italy
Naples
Italy

Editorial Office
MDPI
St. Alban-Anlage 66
4052 Basel, Switzerland

This is a reprint of articles from the Special Issue published online in the open access journal *Future Internet* (ISSN 1999-5903) (available at: https://www.mdpi.com/journal/futureinternet/special_issues/NLE_MTA).

For citation purposes, cite each article independently as indicated on the article page online and as indicated below:

LastName, A.A.; LastName, B.B.; LastName, C.C. Article Title. *Journal Name* **Year**, *Volume Number*, Page Range.

ISBN 978-3-0365-3740-5 (Hbk)
ISBN 978-3-0365-3739-9 (PDF)

Contents

About the Editors vii

Massimo Esposito, Giovanni Luca Masala, Aniello Minutolo and Marco Pota
Special Issue "Natural Language Engineering: Methods, Tasks and Applications"
Reprinted from: *Future Internet* **2022**, *14*, 106, doi:10.3390/fi14040106 1

Seid Muhie Yimam, Abinew Ali Ayele, Gopalakrishnan Venkatesh, Ibrahim Gashaw and Chris Biemann
Introducing Various Semantic Models for Amharic: Experimentation and Evaluation with Multiple Tasks and Datasets
Reprinted from: *Future Internet* **2021**, *13*, 275, doi:10.3390/fi13110275 5

Guizhe Song and Degen Huang
A Sentiment-Aware Contextual Model for Real-Time Disaster Prediction Using Twitter Data
Reprinted from: *Future Internet* **2021**, , 163, doi:10.3390/fi13070163 23

Claudia A. Libbi, Jan Trienes, Dolf Trieschnigg, and Christin Seifert
Generating Synthetic Training Data for Supervised De-Identification of Electronic Health Records
Reprinted from: *Future Internet* **2021**, *13*, 136, doi:10.3390/fi13050136 39

Jie Yu, Yaliu Li, Chenle Pan and Junwei Wang
A Classification Method for Academic Resources Based on a Graph Attention Network
Reprinted from: *Future Internet* **2021**, *13*, 64, doi:10.3390/fi13030064 63

Dario Onorati, Pierfrancesco Tommasino, Leonardo Ranaldi, Francesca Fallucchi and Fabio Massimo Zanzotto
Pat-in-the-Loop: Declarative Knowledge for Controlling Neural Networks
Reprinted from: *Future Internet* **2020**, *12*, 218, doi:10.3390/fi12120218 79

Yana Agafonova, Alexey Tikhonov and Ivan P. Yamshchikov
Paranoid Transformer: Reading Narrative of Madness as Computational Approach to Creativity
Reprinted from: *Future Internet* **2020**, *12*, 182, doi:10.3390/fi12110182 91

About the Editors

Massimo Esposito is senior researcher at the Institute for High Performance Computing and Networking of the National Research Council of Italy. He received a M.Sc. in Computer Science Engineering (Cum Laude) in 2004, a 1st level Master degree in 2007, and a Ph.D. degree in Information Technology Engineering in 2011. Since 2012, he has been a contract professor of Informatics at the University of Naples Federico II. His current research interests are focused on Artificial Intelligence algorithms and techniques, mixing deep learning and knowledge-based technologies, for building intelligent systems able to converse, understand natural language and answer to questions, with emphasis on the distributional neural representation of text, and on specific natural language tasks such as part of speech tagging, sentence classification and open information extraction. He has been involved in different national and European projects, has been on the program committee of many international conferences, and is member of the editorial board of some international journals. He authored over 100 peer-reviewed papers on international journals and conference proceedings.

Marco Pota is researcher at the Institute for High Performance Computing and Networking of the National Research Council of Italy. He received M.Sc. in Chemical Engineering in 2004, and a Ph.D. degree in Multiscale Modelling, Computational Simulation and Characterization for Materials and Life Sciences in 2010. Since 2018, he has been a contract professor of Informatics at the University of Naples Federico II. His current research interests are focused on Artificial Intelligence algorithms and techniques, based on deep learning and knowledge-based technologies, for building predictive models and solving specific natural language processing tasks. He has been involved in different national projects, in the organization of many international conferences, and is guest editor of some international journals. He has authored many peer-reviewed papers on international journals and conference proceedings.

Giovanni Luca Masala is Senior Lecturer in Computer Science at the University of Kent and Leader of the Robotics Lab. Dr. Masala has a Ph.D. in Applied Physics (AI in medical applications) and a Laurea (MSc+BSc) in Electronic Engineering (AI) both at the University of Cagliari, Italy. Dr. Masala has published widely on ranked journals in AI topics. Dr. Masala is a member of several program committees in international conferences, and he is a Guest Editor in AI topics in a number of journals. In the field of natural language understanding, he was part of a small group of international researchers who developed a very large-scale neural network of cognitive and language processing called ANNABELL. The publication in PLoS One in 2015 (1) received high impact both scientifically and in the media. The main interests are brain-inspired architecture for natural language, robotics, human-robot interaction, machine learning on medical applications, and medical imaging.

Aniello Minutolo received the M.Sc. degree in computer science engineering from the University of Naples Federico II and the Ph.D. degree in information technology engineering from the University of Naples Parthenope. Since 2018, he has been a Contract Professor of informatics with the Faculty of Engineering, University of Naples Federico II. He is currently a Researcher with the Institute for High Performance Computing and Networking, National Research Council (ICARCNR), Italy. His current research interests include artificial intelligence, decision support systems, dialog systems, knowledge management, and modeling and reasoning. He has been involved in different national and European projects and on the program committee of some international conferences and workshops. Moreover, he is also a member of the editorial board of some international journals.

Editorial

Special Issue "Natural Language Engineering: Methods, Tasks and Applications"

Massimo Esposito [1], Giovanni Luca Masala [2], Aniello Minutolo [1] and Marco Pota [1,*]

[1] Institute for High Performance Computing and Networking–National Research Council of Italy (ICAR-CNR), 80100 Naples, Italy; massimo.esposito@icar.cnr.it (M.E.); aniello.minutolo@icar.cnr.it (A.M.)
[2] School of Computing, University of Kent, Canterbury CT2 7NZ, UK; g.masala@kent.ac.uk
* Correspondence: marco.pota@icar.cnr.it

Natural language engineering includes a continuously enlarging variety of methods for solving natural language processing (NLP) tasks within a pervasive number of applications. In this field, impressive achievements have been reached recently, by means of systems using deep learning or different approaches, which allowed AI to advance toward human levels in NLP tasks such as translation [1], reading comprehension [2,3], information retrieval [4], and sentiment analysis [5–7], and to build systems for question answering [8–11], conversational systems [12,13], and recommender systems (https://developers.google.com/machine-learning/recommendation, accessed on 24 March 2022).

However, despite the remarkable successes in different NLP tasks, natural language engineering is nowadays a field of research of increasing interest due to the remaining difficulties associated with its comprehension and generation, which are capabilities of humans still not well understood by computer systems from a cognitive perspective. Current difficulties include the complexity of deep learning models, growing in directions chosen empirically [14], the difficulty of scaling them down for implementation on the edge, the scarcity of datasets for some languages (https://www.aclweb.org/portal/content/emnlp-workshop-deep-learning-low-resource-nlp, accessed on 24 March 2022), and the lack of explainability of the models [15].

This Special Issue highlights the most recent research being carried out in the field of NLP methods, to face these open issues, with particular emphasis on emerging approaches for learning interactively or autonomously from data, single and multiple language understanding and grounding for analysis and generation, as well as potential or real applications in different domains and everyday devices.

To this aim, this Special Issue gathers original contributions by researchers with broad expertise in various fields—natural language processing, cognitive science and psychology, artificial intelligence and neural networks, computational modeling and neuroscience—discussing their cutting-edge work as well as perspectives on future directions in the whole range of theoretical and practical aspects, technologies, and systems in this research area.

There are six contributions selected for this Special Issue, representing progress and potential applications in the following NLP areas specifically addressed:

1. **Low-resource natural language processing.** Yimam et al. state that the available pre-trained models do not fit well with the need for low-resource languages; thus, they introduce different semantic models for Amharic and fine-tune two pre-trained models and train seven new models. Moreover, they employ these models for different NLP tasks and study their impact.
2. **Natural language understanding, generation and grounding.** Agafonova et al. revisit the receptive theory in the context of computational creativity; they present a fully autonomous text generation engine with raw output simulating the narrative of

Citation: Esposito, M.; Masala, G.L.; Minutolo, A.; Pota, M. Special Issue "Natural Language Engineering: Methods, Tasks and Applications". *Future Internet* **2022**, *14*, 106. https://doi.org/10.3390/fi14040106

Received: 2 March 2022
Accepted: 23 March 2022
Published: 26 March 2022

a mad digital person and discuss the impact of receptive theory, chance discovery, and simulation of fringe mental state on the understanding of computational creativity.

3. **Neuroscience-inspired cognitive architectures.** Onorati et al. propose a model to control a specific class of syntax-oriented neural networks by adding declarative rules, by exploiting parse trees and subtrees, to include human control in NLP systems, and they show that declarative rules representing human knowledge can be effective for some NLP tasks.
4. **Search and information retrieval.** Yu et al. underline that classification of resource can help the filtering of massive resources, and they propose for this scope an Association Content Graph Attention Network, which is based on association features and content attributes of academic resources, considering both semantic relevance and academic relevance, to improve the accuracy of academic resource classification.
5. **Text de-identification.** Libbi et al. consider the lack of large, annotated Electronic Health Records datasets due to privacy concerns and annotation costs, thus they propose the use of language models for generating artificial data jointly with annotations that can be effectively used, alone or in combination with real data, to train supervised named-entity recognition models for de-identification.
6. **Applications in science, engineering, medicine, healthcare, finance, business, law, education, industry, transportation, retailing, telecommunication and multimedia.** Song and Huang propose to use the massive amount of data generated by social media for disaster analysis, and in particular to use Twitter to track disaster events to make a speedy rescue plan, and for this scope, they propose a sentiment-aware contextual model, consisting of a layer that can generate sentimental contextual embeddings from tweets, a BiLSTM layer with attention, and a 1D convolutional layer for local feature extraction, demonstrating superior performance in Tweets-based disaster analysis.

Acknowledgments: This Special Issue was successful thanks to the valuable contributions of all the authors, the dedicated referees, and the Editorial team of *Future Internet*.

Conflicts of Interest: The authors declare no conflict of interest.

References

1. Tan, Z.; Wang, S.; Yang, Z.; Chen, G.; Huang, X.; Sun, M.; Liu, Y. Neural machine translation: A review of methods, resources, and tools. *AI Open* **2020**, *1*, 5–21. [CrossRef]
2. Guarasci, R.; Minutolo, A.; Damiano, E.; De Pietro, G.; Fujita, H.; Esposito, M. ELECTRA for Neural Coreference Resolution in Italian. *IEEE Access* **2021**, *9*, 115643–115654. [CrossRef]
3. Marulli, F.; Pota, M.; Esposito, M. A comparison of character and word embeddings in bidirectional LSTMs for POS tagging in Italian. In *Intelligent Interactive Multimedia Systems and Services*; De Pietro, G., Gallo, L., Howlett, R.J., Jain, L.C., Vlacic, L., Eds.; Springer: Berlin, Germany, 2019; Volume 98, pp. 14–23.
4. Guarasci, R.; Damiano, E.; Minutolo, A.; Esposito, M.; De Pietro, G. Lexicon-grammar based open information extraction from natural language sentences in Italian. *Expert Syst. Appl.* **2020**, *143*, 112954. [CrossRef]
5. Pota, M.; Ventura, M.; Fujita, H.; Esposito, M. Multilingual evaluation of pre-processing for BERT-based sentiment analysis of tweets. *Expert Syst. Appl.* **2021**, *181*, 115119. [CrossRef]
6. Pota, M.; Esposito, M.; Palomino, M.A.; Masala, G.L. A subword-based deep learning approach for sentiment analysis of political tweets. In Proceedings of the 2018 32nd International Conference on Advanced Information Networking and Applications Workshops (WAINA), Krakow, Poland, 16–18 May 2018.
7. Yadav, A.; Vishwakarma, D.K. Sentiment analysis using deep learning architectures: A review. *Artif. Intell. Rev.* **2020**, *53*, 4335–4385. [CrossRef]
8. Pota, M.; Fuggi, A.; Esposito, M.; De Pietro, G. Extracting Compact Sets of Features for Question Classification in Cognitive Systems: A Comparative Study. In Proceedings of the 2015 10th International Conference on P2P, Parallel, Grid, Cloud and Internet Computing (3PGCIC), Krakow, Poland, 4–6 November 2015.
9. Esposito, M.; Damiano, E.; Minutolo, A.; De Pietro, G.; Fujita, H. Hybrid query expansion using lexical resources and word embeddings for sentence retrieval in question answering. *Inf. Sci.* **2020**, *514*, 88–105. [CrossRef]
10. Pota, M.; Esposito, M.; De Pietro, G.; Fujita, H. Best Practices of Convolutional Neural Networks for Question Classification. *Appl. Sci.* **2020**, *10*, 4710. [CrossRef]
11. Yuan, S.; Zhang, Y.; Tang, J.; Hall, W.; Cabotà, J.B. Expert finding in community question answering: A review. *Artif. Intell. Rev.* **2020**, *53*, 843–874. [CrossRef]

12. Minutolo, A.; Esposito, M.; De Pietro, G. A conversational chatbot based on knowledge-graphs for factoid medical questions. In Proceedings of the 16th International Conference on Intelligent Software Methodologies, Tools and Techniques, KitaKyushu, Japan, 26–28 September 2017.
13. Minutolo, A.; Damiano, E.; De Pietro, G.; Fujita, H.; Esposito, M. A conversational agent for querying Italian Patient Information Leaflets and improving health literacy. *Comput. Biol. Med.* **2021**, *141*, 105004. [CrossRef]
14. Pota, M.; Marulli, F.; Esposito, M.; De Pietro, G.; Fujita, H. Multilingual POS tagging by a composite deep architecture based on character-level features and on-the-fly enriched Word Embeddings. *Knowl. Based Syst.* **2019**, *164*, 309–323. [CrossRef]
15. Zohuri, B.; Moghaddam, M. Deep Learning Limitations and Flaws. *Mod. Approaches Mater. Sci. Short Commun.* **2020**, *2*, 241–250. [CrossRef]

future internet

Article

Introducing Various Semantic Models for Amharic: Experimentation and Evaluation with Multiple Tasks and Datasets

Seid Muhie Yimam [1,*], Abinew Ali Ayele [1,2], Gopalakrishnan Venkatesh [3], Ibrahim Gashaw [4] and Chris Biemann [1]

1 Language Technology Group, Universität Hamburg, Grindelallee 117, 20146 Hamburg, Germany ; abinewaliayele@gmail.com (A.A.A.); christian.biemann@uni-hamburg.de (C.B.)
2 Faculty of Computing, Bahir Dar Institute of Technology, Bahir Dar University, Bahir Dar 6000, Ethiopia
3 International Institute of Information Technology, Bangalore 560100, India; gopalakrishnan.v@iiitb.org
4 College of Informatics, University of Gondar, Gondar 6200, Ethiopia; ibrahimug1@gmail.com
* Correspondence: seid.muhie.yimam@uni-hamburg.de; Tel.: +49-4042-883-2418

Abstract: The availability of different pre-trained semantic models has enabled the quick development of machine learning components for downstream applications. However, even if texts are abundant for low-resource languages, there are very few semantic models publicly available. Most of the publicly available pre-trained models are usually built as a multilingual version of semantic models that will not fit well with the need for low-resource languages. We introduce different semantic models for Amharic, a morphologically complex Ethio-Semitic language. After we investigate the publicly available pre-trained semantic models, we fine-tune two pre-trained models and train seven new different models. The models include Word2Vec embeddings, distributional thesaurus (DT), BERT-like contextual embeddings, and DT embeddings obtained via network embedding algorithms. Moreover, we employ these models for different NLP tasks and study their impact. We find that newly-trained models perform better than pre-trained multilingual models. Furthermore, models based on contextual embeddings from FLAIR and RoBERTa perform better than word2Vec models for the NER and POS tagging tasks. DT-based network embeddings are suitable for the sentiment classification task. We publicly release all the semantic models, machine learning components, and several benchmark datasets such as NER, POS tagging, sentiment classification, as well as Amharic versions of WordSim353 and SimLex999.

Keywords: datasets; neural networks; semantic models; Amharic NLP; low-resource language; text tagging

Citation: Yimam, S.M.; Ayele, A.A.; Venkatesh, G.; Gashaw I.; Biemann C. Introducing Various Semantic Models for Amharic: Experimentation and Evaluation with Multiple Tasks and Datasets. *Future Internet* **2021**, *13*, 275. https://doi.org/10.3390/fi13110275

Academic Editors: Massimo Esposito, Giovanni Luca Masala, Aniello Minutolo and Marco Pota

Received: 11 October 2021
Accepted: 25 October 2021
Published: 27 October 2021

1. Introduction

For the development of applications with semantic capabilities, models such as word embeddings and distributional semantic representations play an important role. These models are the building blocks for a number of natural language processing (NLP) applications. Recently, with the advent of more computing power and the widespread availability of a large number of texts, pre-trained models are becoming commonplace. The availability of pre-trained semantic models allows researchers to focus on the actual NLP task rather than investing time in computing such models. In this work, we consider semantic models as the techniques and approaches used to build word representations or embeddings that can be used in different downstream NLP applications.

The work by [1] indicates that word-level representations or word embeddings have played a central role in the development of many NLP tasks. For a named entity recognition task, there are many works that indicate word2Vec lead to a performance boost [2–5]. Static word-embedding models have been also integrated for several NLP tasks such as sentiment analysis [6,7], part-of-speech (POS) tagging [8,9], semantic composi-tionality

[10,11], and many more. While static word-embedding models fail to capture contextual information regarding ambiguous words, the introduction of BERT [12] and similar models have addressed this limitation. The work by [13] indicates that BERT was able to represent the traditional NLP pipeline in an interpretable way, covering some of the basic NLP tasks such as POS tagging, NER, semantic roles, and co-reference resolution.

Even though getting text data is not a problem for low-resource languages, there are only limited efforts in releasing pre-trained semantic models [14,15]. In the case of Amharic, there are very few pre-trained models, for example fastText [16], XLMR [17], and Multi-Flair [18]. Also, these models are produced as part of multilingual and cross-lingual experimental setups, which will not fit the needs of most NLP tasks [14].

In this paper, we have surveyed the existing NLP tasks for Amharic, including available datasets and trained models. Based on the insights on the current state-of-the-art progress on Amharic NLP, we performed different experiments specifically on the integration of semantic models for various tasks, particularly parts-of-speech (POS) tagging, named entity recognition (NER), sentiment analysis, word relatedness, and similarity computation.

The main contributions of this work are many folds: (1) Surveying the existing NLP tasks and semantic models. (2) Computing and fine-tuning nine semantic models and the release of the models publicly along with benchmark datasets for future research. (3) Investigating the main challenges in the computation and integration of semantic models for the Amharic text. (4) Implementing the first Amharic text segmenter and normalizer component and releasing it along with the models and datasets. (5) Release of the word similarity and relatedness datasets (WordSim353 and SimLex999) that have initially been translated using Google Translate API and subsequently have been validated by native speakers. Table 1 shows the different resources (models, tools, datasets) we have contributed. The different strategies and methods used to collect the different dataset and corpus are presented in Section 1.1.2.

Table 1. Resources (models, preprocessing tools, and models). For existing resources, we have indicated our contributions. * indicated corpus we have gathered from the web using the Scrapy (https://scrapy.org/ (accessed on 24 October 2021)) open source and collaborative Python framework and using the Tweeter API (https://developer.twitter.com/en/docs/ (accessed on 24 October 2021)). ** indicates the models that we have built using the datasets. *** indicates semantic models that are publicly available.

Resource	Description	Remark
NER dataset ***	Benchmark dataset & models	From SAY project
POS dataset ***	Benchmark dataset & models	From previous work [19]
Sentiment dataset	Different models	Our work [20]
word2Vec **	CBOW and SKipgram	Our corpus *
fastText **	CBOW and SKipgram	Our corpus *
fastText ***	CBOW	From fastText
DT models **	Trigram models	Our corpus *
XLRM ***	Transformer model	From Huggingface
MultFlair ***	Contextualized embedding	From FLAIR repository
AmFlair & MultFlairFT **	Contextualized embedding	Fin-tuned our corpus *
AmRoBERTa **	Transformer model	Newly built our corpus *
Pre-processing **	Tokenization & Segmentation	New tools
WordSim & SimLex ****	Word Similarity	Translated from English

1.1. Amharic Language

Amharic is the second most widely-spoken Semitic language (Ethio-Semitic language) after Arabic [21]. It is the working language of the Federal Democratic Republic of Ethiopia and is also the working language of many regional states in the country like Amhara, Addis Ababa, South Nations and Nationalities, Benishangul Gumuz, and Gambella. The language has a considerable number of speakers in all regional states of the country [22].

Amharic is a morphologically-rich language that has its own characterizing phonetic, phonological, and morphological properties [23]. It is a low-resource language without well-developed natural language processing applications and resources.

1.1.1. Pre-Processing and Normalization

Amharic is written in Geez alphabets called Fidel or (ፊደል). In traditional Amharic writing, each word and sentence is supposed to be separated using a unique punctuation mark, namely the Ethiopic comma (፡). However, the modern writing system uses a single space to separate words. Using a single space suffices to split the majority of texts into tokens. However, there are some punctuation marks, such as: (1) The Ethiopic full stop (።) used to mark the end of a sentence. (2) The Ethiopic comma (፡) and the Ethiopic semicolon (፤) that are equivalent to their English counterparts. (3) The Ethiopic question mark (፧) that is used to mark the end of questions in Amharic. Moreover, most people also use Latin punctuation marks such as comma, semicolons, question marks, and exclamation marks, even mixing with the Amharic punctuation marks.

For a properly written Amharic text, splitting sentences can be accomplished using the Amharic end of sentence marks (።), question marks, or exclamation marks. However, it might be also the case that people use two Ethiopic commas or two Latin commas to mark the end of a sentence. In the worst case, the Amharic sentence can be delimited with a verb (placed at the end of the sentence) without putting any punctuation marks. As far as we know, there is no proper tool to tokenize words and segment sentences in Amharic. As part of this work, we make available our Amharic segmenter within the FLAIR framework.

Moreover, some of the "Fidels" in Amharic have different representations, for example, the "Fidel" **ሀ** (ha) can have more than four representations (such as **ሃ**, **ሐ**, **ሓ**, **ኀ**, **ኃ**, and so on). As the Amharic script originates from the Geez script, the use of different Fidels implied a change in meaning. However, the inherent meaning of the different Fidels became irrelevant in modern writing systems, so users can write with the similar-sounding Fidels interchangeably. These lead to texts written, especially in online communication such as news and social media communications, with different writing styles where the different Fidels are used randomly. For NLP processing, an arbitrary representation of words might pose a serious problem, for example the word **ሰው** (man) and **ሠው** (man) might have different embeddings while being the same word. To address this problem, we have built an Amharic text normalization tool that will normalize texts written with different "Fidel" sharing the same sound to a majority class.

1.1.2. Data Sources for Semantic Models

To build distributional semantic models, a large amount of text is required. These days, an enormous amount of texts are being generated continuously from different sources. As we want to build general-purpose semantic models, we collected datasets from different channels, including news portals, social media texts, and general web corpus. For the general web-corpus dataset, we used a focused web crawler to collect Amharic texts. Datasets from the Amharic Web Corpus [24] were also combined to a general-purpose data source. News articles were scraped from January 2020 until May 2020 on a daily basis using the Python Scrappy tool (https://scrapy.org/ (accessed on 24 October 2021)). Similarly, using Twitter and YouTube APIs, we collected tweets and comments written in the 'Fidel' script. In total, 6,151,995 sentences with over 335 million tokens were collected that are used to train the different semantic models.

2. Materials and Methods

In this section, we will discuss the pre-trained semantic models and explain the detailed processes we have followed to fine-tune these models. We will also describe the technologies and approaches we have considered to build new models.

2.1. Distributional Thesaurus

The distributional hypothesis describes that words with similar meanings tend to appear in similar contexts [25], hence it is possible to build distributional thesaurus (DT) automatically from a large set of free texts. In this approach, if words $w1$ and $w2$ both occur with another word $w3$, then $w1$ and $w2$ are assumed to share some common feature. The more features two words share, the more similar they are considered.

- **AmDT** : The DT was built using the JobImText (http://ltmaggie.informatik.uni-hamburg.de/jobimtext/ (accessed on 24 October 2021)) framework [26]. JoBimText is an open-source framework to compute DTs using lexicalized features that supports an automatic text expansion using contextualized distributional similarity.

2.2. Static Word Embeddings

The only pre-trained static word embedding for Amharic text is the **fastText** model, which is trained from Wikipedia and data from the common crawl project [16]. To compare and contrast with the fastText model, we trained a wword2Vec model based on the corpus presented in Section 1.1.2.

- **AmWord2Vec**: Word2Vec [27] helps to learn word representations (word embeddings) that employ a two-layer neural network architecture. Embeddings can be computed using a large set of texts as input to the neural network architecture. The models are built with both the Continuous Bag of Words Model (CBOW) and Skip-gram methods using in 300-dimensional vectors. As seen in Figure 1, the CBOW model considers the conditional probability of generating the central target word from given context words. The Skip-gram approach is the inverse of the CBOW that predicts the context from the target words. We used the Genism Python Library [28] to train the embeddings using the default parameters.
- **fastText**: The pre-trained fastText embeddings distributed by Grave et al. [16] have been trained using a mixture of the Wikipedia and Common Crawl datasets. These 300-dimensional vectors have been trained using Continuous Bag of Words (CBOW) with position-weights, with character n-grams of a length of size 5, a window of size 5, and a negatives sample of size 10.

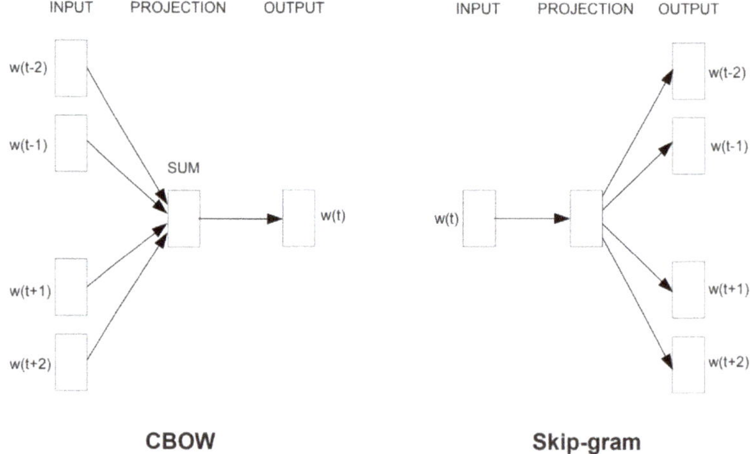

Figure 1. Word2Vec model architecture [27].

2.3. Network Embeddings

Network embeddings allow representing nodes in a graph in the form of low-dimensional representation (embeddings) to maintain the relationship of nodes [29–31].

In this paper, we first compute the network-based distributional thesaurus (AmDT) and later compute the network embeddings from the DT using DeepWalk [32] and Role2Vec [33] algorithms. These two state-of-the-art network embedding algorithms have been selected for this study as they belong to different categories as explained below.

- **DeepWalk**: The latent node embeddings produced by DeepWalk [32] encodes the social representations, like neighborhood similarity and community membership of graph vertices by modeling a stream of truncated random walks.
- **Role2Vec**: The Role2Vec [33] framework introduces the flexible notion of attributed random walks. This provides a basis to generalize the traditional methods, which rely on random walks, to transfer to new nodes and graphs. This is achieved by learning a mapping function between a vertex attribute vector and a role, represented by vertex connectivity patterns, such that two vertices belong to the same role if they are structurally similar or equivalent. The embeddings have been computed using the karateclub [34] Python library. The network embeddings are trained using the hyper-parameter configuration of the package shown in Table 2.

Table 2. Training parameters for the different semantic models and NLP applications.

Model Name	Model Parameters
DeepWalk	128 dimensions, walk number 10, walk length 80, window size is 5
Role2Vec	128 dimensions, walk number 10, walk length 80, window size is 2
MultFlairFT	sequence length of 250, mini batch size of 100, max epochs 10
AmFlair	sequence length of 250, mini batch size of 100, max epochs 10
AmRoBERTa	epochs of 5, per gpu train batch size of 8, block size of 512
SequenceTaggers	hidden size of 256, mini-batch size of 32, epochs of 150

2.4. FLAIR Embeddings

FLAIR embeddings are contextualized embeddings, which are trained based on sequences of characters where words are contextualized by their surrounding texts [35]. Unlike word2Vec embeddings, FLAIR embeddings enable us to compute different representations for the same word based on the surrounding contexts, as shown in Figure 2. In addition to the contextualized word-embeddings computation, the FLAIR framework integrates document embedding functionalities such as *DocumentPoolEmbeddings*, which produces document embeddings from pooled word embeddings and *DocumentLSTMEmbeddings*, which provides document embeddings from LSTM over word embedding [36]. For this experiment, we have considered three semantic models based on the FLAIR contextual string embeddings.

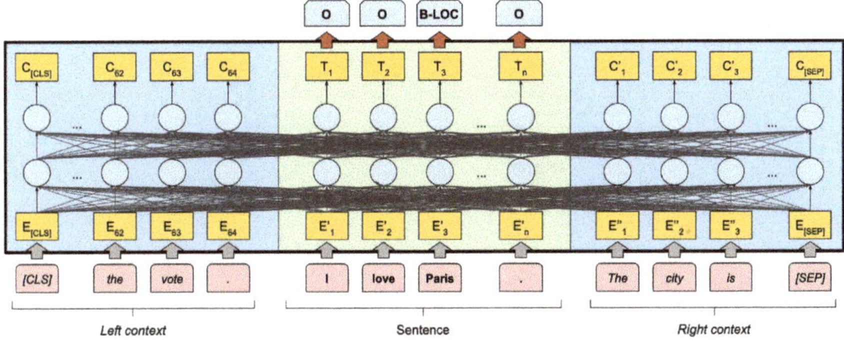

Figure 2. The FLAIR model architecture [37] for document-level features.

- **MultFlair** : As part of the FLAIR embedding models ecosystem, Schweter [18] has built multilingual word embedding using the JW300 corpus [38]. JW300 is compiled from parallel corpora of over 300 languages with around 100,000 parallel sentences per language pair.
- **MultFlairFT**: We have fine-tuned the MultFlair embedding model using our corpus. Fine-tuning the model runs on our GPU server, which was completed in 18 days.
- **AmFlair**: This is a new FLAIR embedding model we have trained from scratch using our corpus. The training is performed on a GPU server (GeForce RTX 2080) with the training parameters shown in Table 2. The training was completed in 6 days.

2.5. Transformer-Based Embeddings

With the release of Google's Bidirectional Encoder Representations from Transformer (BERT) [12], word representation strategies have shifted from the traditional static embeddings to a contextualized embedding representation. While Figure 3 shows the transformer model architecture [39], Figure 4 shows the pre-training and fine-tuning procedures in BERT. BERT-like models have an advantage over static embeddings as they can accommodate different embedding representations for the same word based on its context. In this task, we have used RoBERTa, which is a replication of BERT developed by Facebook [40]. Unlike BERT, RoBERTa removed the *next sentence prediction* functionality to train on longer sequences, dynamically changing the masking patterns.

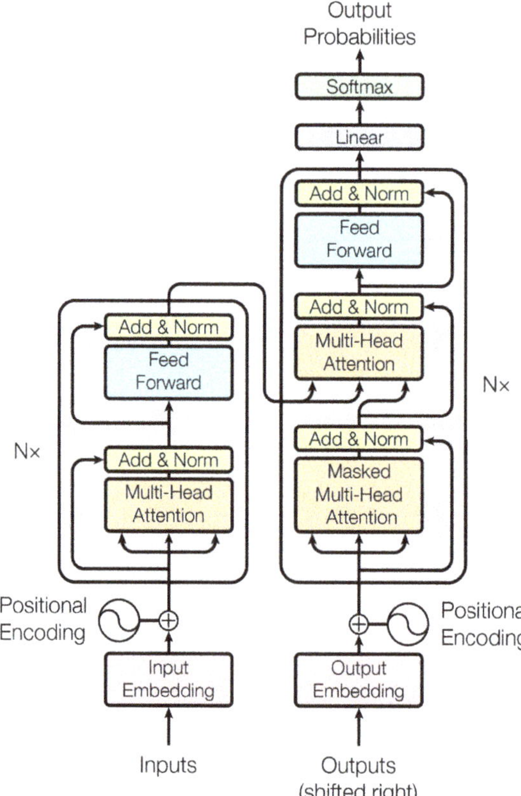

Figure 3. The transformer model architecture [39].

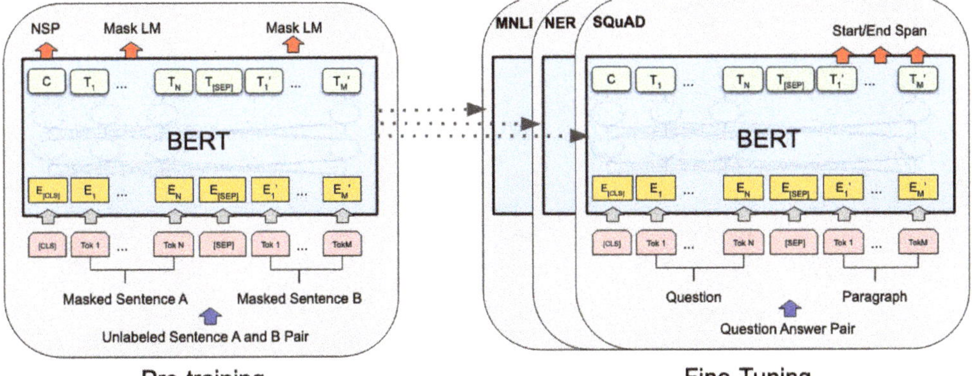

Figure 4. Architecture of the BERT pre-training and fine-tuning procedures [12].

In this experiment, two transformer-based embedding models are used.

- **XLMR**: Unsupervised Cross-lingual Representation Learning at Scale (XLMR) is a generic cross-lingual sentence encoder that is trained on 2.5 TB of newly-created clean CommonCrawl data in 100 languages including Amharic [17].
- **AmRoBERTa:** Is a RoBERTa model that is trained using our corpus, as discussed in Section 1.1.2. It has been trained using 4 GPUs (Quadro RTX 6000 with 24GB RAM) and it has taken 6 days to complete, with parameters shown in Table 2.

3. Results

In this section, we will report the results for different NLP tasks using the existing and newly-built semantic models. We have also compared the differences in using manually-crafted features and embeddings for machine-learning components.

3.1. Most Similar Words and Masked Word Prediction

One of the most prominent operations to perform using static Word2Vec embeddings is to determine the most similar n words for a target word.

As seen from Table 3, most of the top n similar words from fastText are of a bad quality. We observed that this is due to the fact that the text extracted from Wikipedia is smaller in size so that the word occurs in very few sentences. For the word "ox", the top prediction is a wrong candidate that is instantly retrieved from the first entry in Wikipedia, which is a figurative speech (https://bit.ly/2Beuzi2 (accessed on 24 October 2021)).

Table 3. Comparison of word similarities computed using the pre-trained fastText and the AmWord2Vec models. The English glossaries are an approximate as some of the translations will be very long to put in the table, for example, the word **አይከናወኑለትም** can be translated as "they can not be performed for him".

በሬ(ox)		መብላት(eating)	
fastText	**AmWord2Vec**	**fastText**	**AmWord2Vec**
ባላገደደ(tilted)	ፍየል (goat)	ካማራት (want)	መመገብ (feed)
አየህና (see)	ወይፈን (bull)	አይደፍርም (untouchable)	መግዛት (buy)
ይፈንዳ (explodee	ዶሮ (hen)	አይከናወኑለትም (not perform)	ማጠጣት (drink)
ያበጠው (swollen)	በለቅ (donkey)	መጠጣትና (drink)	ማሽተት (smell)
ባልገባ (enter)	ሙክት (goat)	ዳቦን (bread)	መደነስ (dance)
ለሚጎተት (drag)	በግና (sheep)	ፍሬና (fruit)	መሸጥ (sell)
ቀንዱን (horn)	በግ (sheep)	ላምና (cow)	መሽናት (urinate)

Table 3. *Cont.*

በሬ(ox)		መብላት(eating)	
fastText	**AmWord2Vec**	**fastText**	**AmWord2Vec**
ካራጁ (killer)	አህያ (donkey)	የምችል (can)	መጋገር (backe)
አትክልክለው (prohibit)	እደተናገረው (said)	በማጥቃትና (attack)	መቁጠር (count)
ቀንዳምን (horny)	ጥጃ (calf)	መብላትና (eat)	መሸመት (buy)
ተሴት(female)	ቆዳውን (leather)	በእንጀራ (Injera)	መጋት (drink)
አንኮሌ (Fool)	ሰንጋ (ox)	መጥገብ (satisfied)	መጨፈር (dance)
ተላም (cow)	ሲያርስ (plow)	እንደማይወድ (no like)	ለመብላት (eat)
ገደሉን (downhill)	ለምዱን (sheepskin)	የብይ (marbles)	ማጠብ (wash)
ለቀንዳም (horny)	ጅብ (hyena)	ያቃተን (unable)	ማስብ (think)

The BERT-like transformer-based embeddings such as RoBERTa and XLRM also support predicting the *n* most probable words to fill by masking an arbitrary location in a sentence. As shown in Table 4, we compare the results suggested by AmRoBERTa and the suggestions provided by AmDT and AmWord2Vec models. To contrast the predictions using AmRoBERTa, we present the two sentences that are shown in Examples 1 and 2, where we mask a context-dependent word **ትርፍ**, which can be considered as "profit" in the first sentence and "additional" in the second sentence.

Table 4. Comparison of similar words generated from the AmDT, AmWord2Vec, and two contextualized suggestions from AmRoBERTa for the word **ትርፍ**. Columns AmRoBERTaS1 and AmRoBERTaS2 show the the contextual suggestion for the <mask> word from Sentence1 and Sentence2 of Examples 1 and 2.

ትርፍ: 1. profit, 2. additional			
amDT	**amWord2Vec**	**AmRoBERTaS1**	**AmRoBERTaS2**
ገቢ (income)	ገንዘብ (money)	ገንዘብ (money)	አንድ (one)
ጥቅም (advantage)	ገቢ (income)	ገቢ (income)	የሆነ (is)
እርካታ (statsfaction)	ጥቅም (advantage)	እድል (chance)	ብዙ (many)
ውጤት (result)	ዋጋ (price)	ዋጋ (price)	ማንኛውም (any)
ተቀባይነት (acceptance)	ፍጆታ (consumption)	ብር (money)	ሁሉም (all)
ምንዛሪ (exchange)	ትርፉን (additional)	ድጋፍ (support)	ሌላ (other)
ስኬት (success)	ጠቀሜታ (advantage)	ስራ (work)	ሁለት (two)
መፍትሄ (solution)	ምርት (product)	ሀብት (wealth)	ትልቅ (large)
ፋይዳ (advantage)	ገቢም (income)	አቅም (power)	ማንም (anyone)
እፎይታ (relief)	ዋጋም (price)	ድርሻ (share)	ሶስት (three)
ደስታ (happiness)	ፋይዳ (advantage)	ጥቅም (advantage)	አንድም (one)
ፈውስ (medicament)	ገቢው (income)	ግብር (tax)	አብዛኛው (many)

Example 1. : በተለይም ነጋዴዎች በትንሽ ወጪ ብዙ <mask> የማግኘት ዓላማ በመያዝ ውኃን ከወይን ጋር መደባለቅ... Particularly Merchants, to get more <mask> with less expenditure by mixing water with Wine ...

Example 2. : ታክሲዎችና ባጃጆች ከተፈቀደው መጠን በላይ <mask> ሰው መጫን ካላቆሙ ከስራ ውጪ ይደረጋሉ ተባለ። If Taxis and Bajajs do not stop transporting <mask> people than allowed they will be out of a job.

3.2. Word Similarity and Relatedness Tasks

WordSim353 (http://alfonseca.org/eng/research/wordsim353.html (accessed on 24 October 2021)) and SimLex999 (https://fh295.github.io/simlex.html (accessed on 24 October

2021)) are datasets developed to measure semantic similarity and relatedness between terms [41]. WordSim measures semantic relatedness on a rating scale while SimLex is specifically designed to capture the similarity between terms [42]. Word similarity and relatedness can be measured using word embeddings and context embeddings [43,44]. As we do not have these resources for Amharic, we have used the English WordSim353 and SimLex999 datasets to construct the similarity and relatedness resources. To construct the datasets, we translate the WordSim353 and SimLex999 dataset from English to Amharic using the Google translate API. Since the Google translate API for Amharic is not accurate enough, the dataset is verified by two native Amharic speakers. We removed wrongly translated word pairs and multiword expressions from the dataset. These datasets are one of the contributions of this work that will be published publicly.

We have used the different semantic models to measure the similarity and relatedness scores based on the existing benchmark approaches. The experimental setup follows the established strategy of computing the Spearman correlation (ρ) between the cosine similarity of the word vectors or embeddings and the ground truth score [43]. Table 5 presents the results from this quantitative evaluation.

Table 5. Spearman correlation (ρ) and standard deviation (σ) scores on the Amharic Wordsim353 and SimLex999 datasets.

	Spearman Correlation (ρ)		**std (σ)**	
Models	**Wordsim353**	**SimLex999**	**Wordsim353**	**SimLex999**
AmWord2Vec	0.518	0.285	0.247	0.274
fastText	0.434	**0.314**	0.238	0.245
AmFlair	0.444	0.288	0.183	0.208
MultFlairFT	0.447	0.272	0.166	0.189
MultFlair	0.173	0.231	0.085	0.109
AMRoBERTa	0.285	0.202	0.141	0.133
XLMR	0.182	0.183	0.075	0.065
DeepWalk	**0.523**	0.191	**0.279**	**0.308**
Role2Vec	0.448	0.255	0.202	0.233
English datasets state-of-the-art				
	0.828 [45]	0.76 [46]	-	-

From Table 5, we can see that the "DeepWalk" model works better for the WordSim353 dataset while "AmFlair" and "AmWord2Vec" works better for the SimLex999 datasets. Furthermore, the newly-trained as well as the fine-tuned models produce a better result than the pre-trained embeddings ("XLMR" and "MultFliar"). The low standard deviation (σ) results are due to the fact that most of the similarity scores (cosine similarity) between the "word1" and "word2" embeddings are higher. The higher similarity score between the two words is caused by having almost identical embeddings for each of the words, as the embeddings might not be optimized towards the specific tasks. However, we suggest further investigation to check the quality of the embeddings in the pre-trained models. Please note that the results are not directly comparable with the English datasets (Table 5 at the bottom) as we have kept entries where we have direct translation and when the translation does not lead to multi-word expressions.

Moreover, we have conducted some error analysis on the similarity and relatedness results. The following are some of the observations identified.

1. **Translation errors**: We found out that some of the translations are not accurate. For example, the word pairs 'door' and 'doorway' received the same translation in Amharic as "በር".
2. **Equivalence in translation**: The other case we have observed is that some similar/related words received the same translations. For example, the word pairs 'fast' and 'rapid', both are translated as "ፈጣን".

3. **SimLex antonym annotation**: The ground truth annotation scores for the word pairs 'new' and 'ancient' as well as 'tiny' and 'huge' are near zero. However, the cosine similarity produces a negative result as the word pairs are opposite in meaning.
4. **Pre-trained vs. fine-tuned models**: Finetuning the pre-trained models results in a higher similarity (Table 5). For the word pairs 'professor' and 'cucumber' in WordSim353, the ground truth score is 0.31 (10 is a maximum score). The pre-trained 'MultFlair' model results in a wrong (which is higher) similarity score (0.819) but the fine-tuned model results in a smaller score (0.406) near to the ground truth score.

We can also observe that the scores for SimLex999 are lower than the WordSim353 scores. The work by Hill et al. [44] indicated that LexSim999 tasks are challenging for computational models to replicate as the model should capture similarity independently of relatedness association. Moreover, the results on both datasets for Amharic are lowered compared with the English datasets. This can be attributed to several reasons such as: (1) As the translations are not perfect, the ground truth annotation scores should not be used as it is for Amharic pairs, and (2) as Amharic is morphologically complex, the embeddings obtained might be different from the correct lemma of the word. Hence, the pairs should be first lemmatized to the correct dictionary entry before computing the similarity scores. Furthermore, the annotation should be done by Amharic experts to calculate the similarity and relatedness scores.

3.3. *Parts-of-Speech Tagging*

Using a corpus of one-page long Amharic text, Getachew [47] has developed a part of speech tagger using the stochastic Hidden Markov Model approach that can extract major word classes noun, verb, adjective, auxiliary), but fails to determine subcategory constraints such as number, gender, polarity, tense case, definiteness, and unable to learn from new instances. Gambäck et al. [48] have developed an Amharic POS tagger using three different tag-sets. Similarly, Tachbelie and Menzel [49] have prepared 210,000 manually annotated tagged tokens and developed a factored language model using SVM and HMM. Tachbelie et al. [50] have employed a memory-based tagger, which is appropriate for low-resourced languages like Amharic.

Despite the several works on Amharic POS tagging, there is, as far as we know, no publicly available POS tagger model and benchmark dataset that can be used for downstream applications.

For our Amharic POS tagging experimentation, we have trained different POS tagging models using the dataset compiled by Gashaw and Shashirekha [19]. The dataset is comprehensive in the sense that texts from the different genres are incorporated. The dataset from the Ethiopian Language Research Center (ELRC) of Addis Ababa University [51] consists of news articles covering different topics such as sport, economics, politics, etc. amounting to a total of 210,000 words. The ELRC dataset supports 11 basic tags. The work by Gashaw and Shashirekha [19] extends the ELRC dataset by annotating texts from Quranic and Biblical texts (called ELRCQB). In total, 39,000 sentences are annotated for Amharic POS tags using 62 tags. The dataset is split into training, development and testing instances. The development set is used to optimize parameters during training.

Table 6 shows the experimental results using different models. We built two types of models, the Conditional Random Field (CRF) tagging model and the sequence classifier model using the FLAIR deep learning framework. For the CRF model, the "sci-kit-learn-crfsuite" python wrapper of the original CRF implementation is employed (Model **CRF-Suite** in Table 6). The features for the CRF model include (1) the word, previous word, and the next word, (2) prefixes and suffixes with lengths ranging from 1 to 3, and (3) checking if the word is numeric or not. The remaining models are built using the FLAIR sequence classifier based on the different semantic models using the parameters shown in Table 2 with a GPU:GeForce GTX 1080 11GB server.

Table 6. Experimental results for POS tagging (macro-averages). * indicated the stat-of-the-art result of the ELRCQB dataset but the results are not comparable as: (1) The reported result shows only the accuracy, and (2) they are not benchmark datasets.

Model	Precision	Recall	F1
	CRFSuite Word Features		
CRFSuite	**94.78**	**94.81**	**94.74**
	Word Embeddings		
AmWord2Vec	81.41	81.94	81.05
fastText	84.18	84.46	83.94
	Contextual Embeddings		
AmRoBERTa	94.08	94.13	94.08
AmFlair	91.75	91.71	91.69
MultFlairFT	91.19	91.07	91.06
XLMR	94.20	94.17	94.16
MultFlair	89.65	89.53	89.48
	Graph Embeddings		
DeepWalk	82.27	82.71	81.81
Role2Vec	81.45	81.95	80.91
	State-of-the-art result		
		92.27 accuracy *	

3.4. Named Entity Recognition

Named entity recognition (NER) is a process of locating and categorizing proper nouns in text documents into predefined classes like a person, organization, location, time, and numeral expressions [52]. In this regard, one of the early attempts for Amharic NER is the work by Ahmed [53], which is conducted on a corpus of 10,405 tokens. Using the CRF classifier, the research indicated that POS tags, suffixes, and prefixes are important features to detect Amharic named entities. The work by Alemu [54] also conducted similar work on a manually developed corpus of 13,538 words with the Stanford tagging scheme. The work by Tadele [55], an approach for a hybrid Amharic named entity recognition employed a combination of machine learning (decision trees and support vector machines) and rule-based methods. They have reported that the pure machine learning approaches with POS and nominal flag features outperformed the hybrid approach.

Another work by Gambäck and Sikdar [56] also developed language-independent features to extract Amharic named entities using a bi-directional LSTM deep learning neural network model and merged the different feature vectors with word embedding for better performance. Sikdar and Gambäck [57] later employed a stack-based deep learning approach incorporating various semantic information sources that are built using an unsupervised learning algorithm with word2Vec, and a CRF classifier trained with language-independent features. They have reported that the stack-based approach outperformed other deep learning algorithms.

The main challenges with Amharic NER are: (1) As there are no capitalization rules in the language, it is very difficult to build a simple rule or pattern to extract named entities. (2) POS tags might help in discriminating named entities from other tokens, however, there is no publicly-available POS tagger for Amharic that can be integrated into NER systems. (3) Most of the research is carried out as part of academic requirements for a Bachelor's and Master's thesis where the research output was not well documented. Moreover, there are no benchmark dataset or tools that could advance future research in Amharic. In this work, we explore the effectiveness of semantic models for Amharic NER and release both the NER models and the benchmark datasets publicly (in Table 7).

Table 7. Experimental results for NER classification (macro-averages).

Model	Precision	Recall	F1
	CRFSuite Word Features		
CRFSuite	80.88	63.89	71.39
	Word Embeddings		
AmWord2Vec	68.11	57.47	62.34
fastText	79.01	55.56	65.24
	Contextual Embeddings		
AmRoBERTa	25.62	30.56	27.87
AmFlair	79.70	74.31	76.91
MultFlairFT	**81.21**	**74.31**	**77.61**
MultFlair	75.58	61.81	68.00
	Graph Embeddings		
DeepWalk	73.95	64.06	68.65
Role2Vec	74.00	60.76	66.73

For this experiment, the Amharic dataset annotated within the SAY project at New Mexico State University's Computing Research Laboratory was used. The data is annotated with six classes, namely person, location, organization, time, title, and others. There are a total of 4237 sentences where 5480 tokens out of 109,676 tokens are annotated as named entities. The dataset is represented in XML format (for the different named entity classes) and is openly available in GitHub (https://github.com/geezorg/data/tree/master/amharic/tagged/nmsu-say (accessed on 24 October 2021)). The same approach as the POS tagger systems was used to train the NER models.

3.5. Sentiment Analysis

The task of sentiment analysis for low-resource languages like Amharic remains challenging due to the lack of publicly available datasets and the unavailability of required NLP tools. Moreover, there are no attempts of analyzing the complexities of sentiment analysis on social media texts (e.g., Twitter dataset), as the contents are highly context-dependent and influenced by the user experience [58]. Some of the existing works in Amharic either target the generation of sentiment lexicon or are limited to the manual analysis of very small social media texts.

The work of Alemneh et al. [59] focuses on the generation of Amharic sentiment lexicon using the English sentiment lexicon. The English lexicon entries are translated to Amharic using a bilingual English-Amharic dictionary.

The work by Gebremeskel [60] builds a rule-based sentiment polarity classification system. Using movie reviews, 955 sentiment lexicon entries are generated. The system is built to detect the presence and absence of the positive and negative sentiment lexicon entries to classify the polarity of the document.

For this work, we considered the recently released sentiment classification datasets, a total of 9400 k tweets where each tweet is annotated by three users [20]. The tweets are sampled using the extended sentiment lexicons from Gebremeskel [60] (to a total of 1194 lexicon entries). We split the dataset into training, testing, and development sets with the 80:10:10 splitting strategy.

We built document-based sentiment classifiers using the different semantic models. For a classical classification approach, we used the term frequency-inverse document frequency (TF-IDF) features using different algorithms from the sci-kit-learn Python machine learning framework. For the deep learning approach, we used the TextClassifier document classification model from the FLAIR framework, which uses the *DocumentRNNEmbeddings* computed from the different word embeddings. Table 8 shows the different experimental results.

Table 8. Experimental results of the test sets on the sentiment classes: "Positive", "Negative" and "Neutral" (macro-averages).

Model	Precision	Recall	F1
	TF-IDF representation		
LogReg	46.80	60.88	52.92
RanfomF	44.59	52.17	48.09
KNN	49.85	50.22	50.03
NearestC	47.36	49.20	48.26
SVM	35.44	46.42	40.20
	Word Embeddings		
AmWord2Vec	55.54	54.91	55.22
fastText	43.50	67.81	53.00
	Contextual Embeddings		
AmFlair	53.24	59.25	56.09
MultFlair	46.96	55.05	50.68
MultFlairFT	54.49	59.58	56.92
AmRoBERTa	46.62	56.39	51.04
	Graph Embeddings		
DeepWalk	55.89	57.71	56.78
Role2Vec	**56.26**	**60.89**	**58.48**
	Baselines		
Stratified	33.79	33.80	33.80
Uniform	29.72	30.96	30.33
MostFreq	33.33	17.31	22.78

4. Discussion

In this section, we will briefly discuss the effects of the different semantic models for the respective NLP tasks.

- **Top *n* similar words**: For the top *n* similar words experiment, as seen from Table 3, the fastText model seems to produce irrelevant suggestions compared to the AmWord2Vec model, which is associated with the smaller corpus size used to train fastText. If we search the predicted word provided by fastText on the Amharic Wikipedia page, we can see that the word co-occurs with the target word only on one occasion. However, as we did not train a new fastText model from scratch using our dataset, we can not claim if the suggestions are mainly due to the size of the dataset or due to the training approach used in fastText architecture.

The similar words suggested by AmDT, AmWord2Vec, and DeepWalk are comparable (see Table 3 and 9). In general, the suggestions from AmDT are more fitting than the ones generated using AmWord2Vec, but the suggestions from AmDT and DeepWalk are equally prevalent to the target words. This corresponds to the finding that the conversion of DTs to a low-level representation can easily be integrated into different applications that rely on word embeddings [61].

Table 9. Comparison of similar words generated from the AmDT and network embedding (Deepwalk) representations.

በሬ(ox)		መብላት(eating)	
AmDT	**DeepWalk**	**AmDT**	**DeepWalk**
በሬ (ox)	ፍየል (goat)	መብላት (eating)	መመገብ (feeding)
በግ (sheep)	በግ (sheep)	መመገብ (feeding)	መጠጣት (drinking)
ከብት (cattle)	ከብት (cattle)	መኖር (living)	መተኛት (sleeping
ዶሮ (hen)	እንስሳ (animal)	መጫወት (playing)	መሸጥ (selling)
ፍየል (goat)	ጅብ (hyena)	መስራት (working)	ማደር (sleeping)
እንስሳ (animal)	አይጥ (mouse)	መስጠት (giving)	መግዛት (buying
ፈረስ (horse)	እባብ (snake)	መሸጥ (selling)	ማምረት (producing
አህያ (donkey)	ዝሆን (elephant)	መነጋገር (talking	ማስቀመጥ (putting)
ሰንጋ (steer)(	ሬሳ (corse)	መንቀሳቀስ (moving)	መውሰድ (taking
በሬዎች (oxen)	ዶሮ (hen)	መግባት (entering)	ማልቀስ (crying)
ሰው (man)	እንቁላል (egg)	ማከናወን (accomplishing)	መትከል (planting)
እባብ (snake)	ስጋ (meat)	መሰብሰብ (collecting)	መተንፈስ (breazing)
ስጋ (meat)	ቅቤ (butter)	መጻፍ (writing)	መጥራት (calling)
ላም (cow)	ፈረስ (horse)	መጠጣት (drinking)	መጫወት (playing)
እርሻ (farm)	ውሻ (dog)	መጓዝ (traveling)	መቁጠር (counting)
አንበሳ (lion)	አህያ (donkey)	መጠቀም (using)	መጮህ (screaming)
ውሻ (dog)	ስጋውን (meat)	መውጣት (going out)	ማውጠቱ (taking out)
በሬውን (ox)	ሳር (grass)	መውሰድ (taking)	መተው (leaving)
ካህን (pastor)	ዝንጀሮ (monkey)	ማገልገል (serving)	ማተኮር (concentrating)
በበሬ (ox)	ዛፍ (tree)	መምራት (leading)	መገናኘት (meeting)

However, the similar words predicted by the DT and word2Vec embeddings are static and it is up to the downstream application to discern the correct word that fits the context. However the next word prediction using the transformer-based models, in this case from the AmRoBERTa model, predicts words that can fit the context. From Examples 1 and 2, we can see that the "masked" words are to be predicted in the two sentences. The two sentences are extracted from the online Amharic news channel (https://www.ethiopianreporter.com/ (accessed on 24 October 2021)) and we masked the word **ትርፍ** in both sentences. In the first sentence (S1), it refers to "profit" while in the second sentence (S2), it intends "additional" or "more". We can see from Table 4 that the AmRoBERTa model generated words that can fit the context of the sentence. We have also observed that AmRoBERTa helps in word completions tasks, which is particularly important for languages such as Amharic, as it is morphologically complex.

- **Word similarity/relatedness**: For the WordSim353 word pair similarity/relatedness experiment, the "DeepWalk" and "AmWord2Vec" models produce the best results. While this is the first dataset and experiment for the Amharic, the Spearman's correlation (ρ) result is better than most of the knowledge-based results for the English counterpart datasets. The state-of-the-art result for English reaches a score of 0.828, which is much larger than the results for Amharic scores. We could not compare the results for several reasons such as (1) errors that occurred during translation and (2) the ground truth annotation scores are directly taken from the English dataset, which might not be optimal. In the future, we suggest to re-annotate the datasets using Amharic experts. We have also observed that the Simlex999 datasets are challenging for the similarity computation task. The "fastText" model achieves better results compared to the other Amharic semantic models. Pre-trained models achieve the lowest results as we can witness from the lower standard deviation (σ) scores.
- **POS tagging**: As seen in Table 6, the semantic models from the transformer-based embeddings perform as good as the CRF algorithm for the POS tagging task. While training the deep learning models took much longer than the CRF algorithm, using deep learning models avoids the need to identify features manually. Both AmRoBERTa and CRF-based models predict the conjunctions, interjections, and prepositions correctly. However, for the rare tags (that occurs fewer times), such as ADJPCS (Adjective with prep. & conj. singular) and VPSs (Verb with prep. singular), AmRoBERTa predicts the

nearest popular tag. However it was observed that CRF perfectly memorizes the correct tag. For example, the word **ኢንዶያግኙ**, which should be a spelling error (maybe the last *s* stands for spelling error inVPSs), is tagged as VPS with AmRoBERTa. We have also observed that the FLAIR contextual embeddings perform very well compared to the network embedding models. The new Amharic FLAIR embeddings (**AmFlair**) and the fine-tuned models (**MultFlairFT**) produce a slightly better result than the publicly-available multilingual FLAIR (**MultFlair** embeddings).

- **Named entity recognition**: In the case of the named entity recognition task, the transformer model performs poorly compared to the CRF and FLAIR embedding models. The FLAIR contextual string embeddings perform better than the word2Vec and network embedding models. We can also observe that AmFlair and MultFlairFT , which are trained and fine-tuned on our dataset, presents better results than the pre-trained MultFlair embeddings model. The XLM transformer-embedding could not produce meaningful predictions (all words are predicted as "Other"). The low performance reported indicates that NER for Amharic is a difficult task. This is due to the fact that named entities do not have distinctive characteristics such as capitalization. Named entities in Amharic are also derived mostly from proper nouns (**አበባ** - flower), from verbs (**አበሩ** - shined), and from adjectives (**ጐበዜ** - clever).
- **Sentiment analysis**: For the sentiment analysis task, we have observed that the deep learning approach outperforms the different classical supervised classifiers. Unlike the NER and the POS tagging tasks, the deep learning approach based on the network embeddings, specifically the **Role2Vec** approach outperforms the other models. Based on our error analysis, we found out that sentiment analysis is challenging both for users and machines as the meaning of the tweet depends on a specific context. Moreover, metaphorical speech and sarcasm are very common in Amharic text, especially on the Twitter dataset, which makes automatic classification very difficult.

In general, we can see that the different semantic models impact various tasks. One semantic model will not fit the need of multiple NLP applications. Another observation is that fine-tuning models or building models with a corpus that is carefully crafted have a better impact on the specific tasks. We believe that the models we publish will help in the development of different NLP applications. It will also open a different research direction to conduct more advanced research as well as to carry out insightful analysis in the usage of semantic models for Amharic NLP.

5. Conclusions

In this work, we presented the first comprehensive study of semantic models for Amharic. We first surveyed the limited number of pre-trained semantic models available, which are provided as part of multilingual experiments. We built different semantic models using text corpora collected from various sources such as online news articles, web corpus, and social media texts. The semantic models we built include (1) word2Vec embeddings, (2) distributional thesaurus models, (3) contextualized string embeddings, (4) distributional thesaurus embedding obtained via network embedding algorithms, and (5) contextualized word embeddings. Furthermore, the publicly available pre-trained semantic models are fine-tuned using our text corpora.

We also experimented with five different NLP tasks to see the effectiveness and limitations of the various semantic models. Our experimental result showed that deep learning models trained with the different semantic representations outperformed the classical machine learning approaches. We publicly released all the nine semantic models, the machine learning models for the different tasks, and benchmark datasets to further advance the research in Amharic NLP .

Author Contributions: Conceptualization, S.M.Y.; methodology, S.M.Y. and A.A.A.; software, S.M.Y. and G.V.; validation, S.M.Y., A.A.A., I.G. and G.V.; formal analysis, S.M.Y., A.A.A. and G.V.; investigation, S.M.Y., I.G. and G.V.; resources, S.M.Y. and G.V.; data curation, S.M.Y., I.G. and G.V.; writing—original draft preparation, S.M.Y.; writing—C.B., S.M.Y. and A.A.A.; visualization, G.V.; supervision, C.B.; project administration, S.M.Y.; funding acquisition, C.B. All authors have read and agreed to the published version of the manuscript.

Funding: This research received no external funding.

Data Availability Statement: The resources such as benchmark NLP datasets for Amharic (PoS tagged dataset, NER annotated dataset, Sentiment dataset, Semantic similarity datasets), Preprocessing and segmentation tools, source codes for the model training, the Amharic corpus will be released in our GitHub repository (https://github.com/uhh-lt/amharicmodels (accessed on 24 October 2021)). The RoBERTa model will be published to the Hugginface repository (https://huggingface.co/uhhlt (accessed on 24 October 2021)). The FLIAR models will be released to the FLAIR list of public libraries.

Conflicts of Interest: The authors declare no conflict of interest.

References

1. Camacho-Collados, J.; Pilehvar, M.T. Embeddings in Natural Language Processing. In Proceedings of the 28th International Conference on Computational Linguistics: Tutorial Abstracts, Online, 12–13 December 2020; pp. 10–15; [CrossRef]
2. Katharina Sienčnik, S. Adapting word2vec to Named Entity Recognition. In Proceedings of the 20th Nordic Conference of Computational Linguistics (NODALIDA 2015), Vilnius, Lithuania, 11–13 May 2015; pp. 239–243.
3. Joshi, M.; Hart, E.; Vogel, M.; Ruvini, J.D. Distributed Word Representations Improve NER for e-Commerce. In Proceedings of the 1st Workshop on Vector Space Modeling for Natural Language Processing, Denver, CO, USA, 31 May–5 June 2015; pp. 160–167; [CrossRef]
4. Hou, J.; Koppatz, M.; Quecedo, J.M.H.; Yangarber, R. Projecting named entity recognizers without annotated or parallel corpora. In Proceedings of the 22nd Nordic Conference on Computational Linguistics, Turku, Finland, 30 September–2 October 2019; pp. 232–241.
5. Mbouopda, M.F.; Yonta, P.M. A Word Representation to Improve Named Entity Recognition in Low-resource Languages. In Proceedings of the 2019 Sixth International Conference on Social Networks Analysis, Management and Security (SNAMS), Granada, Spain, 22–25 October 2019; pp. 333–337; [CrossRef]
6. Barhoumi, A.; Camelin, N.; Aloulou, C.; Estève, Y.; Hadrich Belguith, L. Toward Qualitative Evaluation of Embeddings for Arabic Sentiment Analysis. In Proceedings of the 12th Language Resources and Evaluation Conference, Marseille, France, 13–15 May 2020; pp. 4955–4963.
7. Al-Saqqa, S.; Awajan, A. The Use of Word2vec Model in Sentiment Analysis: A Survey. In Proceedings of the 2019 International Conference on Artificial Intelligence, Robotics and Control, Cairo, Egypt, 14–16 December 2019; pp. 39–43; [CrossRef]
8. Younes, A.; Weeds, J. Embed More Ignore Less (EMIL): Exploiting Enriched Representations for Arabic NLP. In Proceedings of the Fifth Arabic Natural Language Processing Workshop, Barcelona, Spain, 12 December 2020; pp. 139–154.
9. Thavareesan, S.; Mahesan, S. Word embedding-based Part of Speech tagging in Tamil texts. In Proceedings of the 2020 IEEE 15th International Conference on Industrial and Information Systems (ICIIS), Rupnagar, India, 26–28 November 2020; pp. 478–482; [CrossRef]
10. Pickard, T. Comparing word2vec and GloVe for Automatic Measurement of MWE Compositionality. In Proceedings of the Joint Workshop on Multiword Expressions and Electronic Lexicons, Online, 13 December 2020; pp. 95–100.
11. Jadi, G.; Claveau, V.; Daille, B.; Monceaux, L. Evaluating Lexical Similarity to build Sentiment Similarity. In Proceedings of the Tenth International Conference on Language Resources and Evaluation (LREC'16), Portorož, Slovenia, 23–28 May 2016; pp. 1196–1201.
12. Devlin, J.; Chang, M.W.; Lee, K.; Toutanova, K. BERT: Pre-training of Deep Bidirectional Transformers for Language Understanding. In Proceedings of the 2019 Conference of the North American Chapter of the Association for Computational Linguistics: Human Language Technologies, Minneapolis, MN, USA, 2–7 June 2019; Volume 1, pp. 4171–4186.
13. Tenney, I.; Das, D.; Pavlick, E. BERT Rediscovers the Classical NLP Pipeline. In Proceedings of the 57th Annual Meeting of the Association for Computational Linguistics, Florence, Italy, 28 July–2 August 2019; pp. 4593–4601; [CrossRef]
14. Agerri, R.; Vicente, I.S.; Campos, J.A.; Barrena, A.; Saralegi, X.; Soroa, A.; Agirre, E. Give your Text Representation Models some Love: The Case for Basque. *arXiv* **2020**, arXiv:2004.00033.
15. Ulčar, M.; Robnik-Šikonja, M. High Quality ELMo Embeddings for Seven Less-Resourced Languages. *arXiv* **2019**, arXiv:1911.10049.
16. Grave, E.; Bojanowski, P.; Gupta, P.; Joulin, A.; Mikolov, T. Learning Word Vectors for 157 Languages. In Proceedings of the International Conference on Language Resources and Evaluation (LREC 2018), Miyazaki, Japan 7–12 May 2018; pp. 3483–3487.

17. Conneau, A.; Khandelwal, K.; Goyal, N.; Chaudhary, V.; Wenzek, G.; Guzmán, F.; Grave, E.; Ott, M.; Zettlemoyer, L.; Stoyanov, V. Unsupervised Cross-lingual Representation Learning at Scale. In Proceedings of the 58th Annual Meeting of the Association for Computational Linguistics, Online, 5–10 July 2020; pp. 8440–8451.
18. Schweter, S. Multilingual Flair Embeddings. 2020. Available online: https://github.com/flairNLP/flair-lms (accessed on 24 October 2021).
19. Gashaw, I.; Shashirekha, H.L. Machine Learning Approaches for Amharic Parts-of-speech Tagging. *arXiv* **2020**, arXiv:2001.03324.
20. Yimam, S.M.; Alemayehu, H.M.; Ayele, A.; Biemann, C. Exploring Amharic Sentiment Analysis from Social Media Texts: Building Annotation Tools and Classification Models. In Proceedings of the 28th International Conference on Computational Linguistics, Barcelona, Spain, 8–13 December 2020; pp. 1048–1060; [CrossRef]
21. Gezmu, A.M.; Seyoum, B.E.; Gasser, M.; Nürnberger, A. Contemporary Amharic Corpus: Automatically Morpho-Syntactically Tagged Amharic Corpus. In Proceedings of the First Workshop on Linguistic Resources for Natural Language Processing, August 2018; pp. 65–70. Available online: https://aclanthology.org/W18-3809.pdf (accessed on 24 October 2021).
22. Salawu, A.; Aseres, A. Language policy, ideologies, power and the Ethiopian media. *Communicatio* **2015**, *41*, 71–89. [CrossRef]
23. Gasser, M. HornMorpho: A system for morphological processing of Amharic, Oromo, and Tigrinya. In Proceedings of the Conference on Human Language Technology for Development, Alexandria, Egypt, 2–5 May 2011; pp. 94–99.
24. Suchomel, V.; Rychlý, P. *Amharic Web Corpus*; LINDAT/CLARIN Digital Library at the Institute of Formal and Applied Linguistics (ÚFAL), Faculty of Mathematics and Physics, Charles University: Staré Město, Czechia, 2016.
25. Harris, Z.S. Distributional Structure. *Word* **1954**, *10*, 146–162. [CrossRef]
26. Ruppert, E.; Kaufmann, M.; Riedl, M.; Biemann, C. JoBimViz: A Web-based Visualization for Graph-based Distributional Semantic Models. In Proceedings of the ACL-IJCNLP 2015 System Demonstrations, Beijing, China, 26–31 July 2015; pp. 103–108.
27. Mikolov, T.; Sutskever, I.; Chen, K.; Corrado, G.; Dean, J. Distributed representations of words and phrases and their compositionality. *arXiv* **2013**, arXiv:1310.4546.
28. Řehůřek, R.; Sojka, P. Gensim—Statistical Semantics in Python. In Proceedings of the EuroScipy 2011. Available online: https://www.fi.muni.cz/usr/sojka/posters/rehurek-sojka-scipy2011.pdf (accessed on 24 October 2021).
29. Hamilton, W.L.; Ying, R.; Leskovec, J. Representation Learning on Graphs: Methods and Applications. *arXiv* **2017**, arXiv:1709.05584.
30. Sevgili, Ö.; Panchenko, A.; Biemann, C. Improving Neural Entity Disambiguation with Graph Embeddings. In Proceedings of the 57th Annual Meeting of the Association for Computational Linguistics: Student Research Workshop, Florence, Italy, 29 July–1 August 2019; pp. 315–322.
31. Cai, H.; Zheng, V.W.; Chang, K.C.C. A Comprehensive Survey of Graph Embedding: Problems, Techniques, and Applications. *IEEE Trans. Knowl. Data Eng.* **2018**, *30*, 1616–1637. [CrossRef]
32. Perozzi, B.; Al-Rfou, R.; Skiena, S. DeepWalk: Online Learning of Social Representations. In Proceedings of the 20th ACM SIGKDD International Conference on Knowledge Discovery and Data Mining, New York, NY, USA, 24–27 August 2014; pp. 701–710.
33. Ahmed, N.K.; Rossi, R.A.; Lee, J.B.; Willke, T.L.; Zhou, R.; Kong, X.; Eldardiry, H. role2vec: Role-Based Network Embeddings. 2019; pp. 1–7. Available online: http://ryanrossi.com/pubs/role2vec-DLG-KDD.pdf (accessed on 24 October 2021).
34. Rozemberczki, B.; Kiss, O.; Sarkar, R. An API Oriented Open-source Python Framework for Unsupervised Learning on Graphs. *arXiv* **2020**, arXiv:2003.04819.
35. Akbik, A.; Blythe, D.; Vollgraf, R. Contextual String Embeddings for Sequence Labeling. In Proceedings of the 27th International Conference on Computational Linguistics, Santa Fe, NM, USA, 21–25 August 2018; pp. 1638–1649.
36. Akbik, A.; Bergmann, T.; Blythe, D.; Rasul, K.; Schweter, S.; Vollgraf, R. FLAIR: An Easy-to-Use Framework for State-of-the-Art NLP. In Proceedings of the 2019 Conference of the North American Chapter of the Association for Computational Linguistics (Demonstrations), Minneapolis, MN, USA, 2–7 June 2019; pp. 54–59.
37. Schweter, S.; Akbik, A. FLERT: Document-Level Features for Named Entity Recognition. *arXiv* **2020**, arXiv:2011.06993.
38. Agić, Ž.; Vulić, I. JW300: A Wide-Coverage Parallel Corpus for Low-Resource Languages. In Proceedings of the 57th Annual Meeting of the Association for Computational Linguistics, Florence, Italy, 28 July–2 August 2019; pp. 3204–3210.
39. Vaswani, A.; Shazeer, N.; Parmar, N.; Uszkoreit, J.; Jones, L.; Gomez, A.N.; Kaiser, L.U.; Polosukhin, I. Attention is All you Need. In *Advances in Neural Information Processing Systems*; Guyon, I., Luxburg, U.V., Bengio, S., Wallach, H., Fergus, R., Vishwanathan, S., Garnett, R., Eds.; Curran Associates, Inc.: Red Hook, NY, USA, 2017; Volume 30.
40. Liu, Y.; Ott, M.; Goyal, N.; Du, J.; Joshi, M.; Chen, D.; Levy, O.; Lewis, M.; Zettlemoyer, L.; Stoyanov, V. RoBERTa: A Robustly Optimized BERT Pretraining Approach. *arXiv* **2019**, arXiv:1907.11692.
41. Agirre, E.; Alfonseca, E.; Hall, K.; Kravalova, J.; Paşca, M.; Soroa, A. A Study on Similarity and Relatedness Using Distributional and WordNet-based Approaches. In Proceedings of the Human Language Technologies: The 2009 Annual Conference of the North American Chapter of the Association for Computational Linguistics, Boulder, CO, USA, 31 May–5 June 2009; pp. 19–27.
42. Netisopakul, P.; Wohlgenannt, G.; Pulich, A. Word similarity datasets for Thai: Construction and evaluation. *IEEE Access* **2019**, *7*, 142907–142915. [CrossRef]
43. Asr, F.T.; Zinkov, R.; Jones, M. Querying word embeddings for similarity and relatedness. In Proceedings of the 2018 Conference of the North American Chapter of the Association for Computational Linguistics: Human Language Technologies, New Orleans, LA, USA, 1–6 June 2018; Volume 1, pp. 675–684.

44. Hill, F.; Reichart, R.; Korhonen, A. Simlex-999: Evaluating semantic models with (genuine) similarity estimation. *Comput. Linguist.* **2015**, *41*, 665–695. [CrossRef]
45. Speer, R.; Chin, J.; Havasi, C. ConceptNet 5.5: An Open Multilingual Graph of General Knowledge. In Proceedings of the Thirty-First AAAI Conference on Artificial Intelligence, San Francisco, CA, USA, 4–9 February 2017; pp. 4444–4451.
46. Recski, G.; Iklódi, E.; Pajkossy, K.; Kornai, A. Measuring Semantic Similarity of Words Using Concept Networks. In Proceedings of the 1st Workshop on Representation Learning for NLP, Berlin, Germany, 11 August 2016; pp. 193–200; [CrossRef]
47. Getachew, M. Automatic Part-of-Speech Tagging for Amharic Language an Experiment Using Stochastic Hidden Markov Approach. Master's Thesis, School of Graduate Studies, Addis Ababa University, Addis Ababa, Ethiopia, 2001.
48. Gambäck, B.; Olsson, F.; Alemu Argaw, A.; Asker, L. Methods for Amharic Part-of-Speech Tagging. In Proceedings of the First Workshop on Language Technologies for African Languages, Athens, Greece, 31 March 2009; pp. 104–111.
49. Tachbelie, M.Y.; Menzel, W. Amharic Part-of-Speech Tagger for Factored Language Modeling. In Proceedings of the International Conference RANLP-2009, Borovets, Bulgaria, 14–16 September 2009; pp. 428–433.
50. Tachbelie, M.Y.; Abate, S.T.; Besacier, L. Part-of-speech tagging for underresourced and morphologically rich languages—The case of Amharic. *HLTD* **2011** , 50–55. Available online: https://www.cle.org.pk/hltd/pdf/HLTD201109.pdf (accessed on 24 October 2021).
51. Demeke, G.; Getachew, M. *Manual Annotation of Amharic News Items with Part-of-Speech Tags and Its Challenges*. ELRC Working Paper; 2006; Volume 2, pp. 1–16. Available online: https://www.bibsonomy.org/bibtex/d2fa6b0ccf8737fb4046c3d13f274894#export%7D%7B (accessed on 24 October 2021).
52. Zitouni, I. *Natural Language Processing of Semitic Languages*; Springer: Berlin/Heidelberg, Germany, 2014.
53. Ahmed, M. Named Entity Recognition for Amharic Language. Master's Thesis, Addis Ababa University, Addis Ababa, Ethiopia, 2010.
54. Alemu, B. A Named Entity Recognition for Amharic. Master's Thesis, Addis Ababa University, Addis Ababa, Ethiopia, 2013.
55. Tadele, M. Amharic Named Entity Recognition Using a Hybrid Approach. Master's Thesis, Addis Ababa University, Addis Ababa, Ethiopia, 2014.
56. Gambäck, B.; Sikdar, U.K. Named entity recognition for Amharic using deep learning. In Proceedings of the 2017 IST-Africa Week Conference (IST-Africa), Windhoek, Namibia, 31 May–2 June 2017; pp. 1–8.
57. Sikdar, U.K.; Gambäck, B. Named Entity Recognition for Amharic Using Stack-Based Deep Learning. In Proceedings of the International Conference on Computational Linguistics and Intelligent Text Processing, Budapest, Hungary, 17–23 April 2017; pp. 276–287.
58. Gangula, R.R.R.; Mamidi, R. Resource creation towards automated sentiment analysis in Telugu (a low resource language) and integrating multiple domain sources to enhance sentiment prediction. In Proceedings of the Eleventh International Conference on Language Resources and Evaluation (LREC 2018), Miyazaki, Japan, 7–12 May 2018; pp. 627 – 634.
59. Alemneh, G.N.; Rauber, A.; Atnafu, S. Dictionary Based Amharic Sentiment Lexicon Generation. In Proceedings of the International Conference on Information and Communication Technology for Development for Africa, Bahir Dar, Ethiopia, 22–24 November 2019; pp. 311–326.
60. Gebremeskel, S. Sentiment Mining Model for Opinionated Amharic Texts. Available online: http://etd.aau.edu.et/handle/123456789/3029 (accessed on 24 October 2021).
61. Jana, A.; Goyal, P. Can Network Embedding of Distributional Thesaurus Be Combined with Word Vectors for Better Representation? In Proceedings of the 2018 Conference of the North American Chapter of the Association for Computational Linguistics: Human Language Technologies, New Orleans, LA, USA, 1–6 June 2018; Volume 1, pp. 463–473.

future internet

MDPI

Article

A Sentiment-Aware Contextual Model for Real-Time Disaster Prediction Using Twitter Data

Guizhe Song * and Degen Huang

School of Computer Science and Technology, Dalian University of Technology, Dalian 116024, China; huangdg@dlut.edu.cn
* Correspondence: guizhesong@mail.dlut.edu.cn

Abstract: The massive amount of data generated by social media present a unique opportunity for disaster analysis. As a leading social platform, Twitter generates over 500 million Tweets each day. Due to its real-time characteristic, more agencies employ Twitter to track disaster events to make a speedy rescue plan. However, it is challenging to build an accurate predictive model to identify disaster Tweets, which may lack sufficient context due to the length limit. In addition, disaster Tweets and regular ones can be hard to distinguish because of word ambiguity. In this paper, we propose a sentiment-aware contextual model named SentiBERT-BiLSTM-CNN for disaster detection using Tweets. The proposed learning pipeline consists of SentiBERT that can generate sentimental contextual embeddings from a Tweet, a Bidirectional long short-term memory (BiLSTM) layer with attention, and a 1D convolutional layer for local feature extraction. We conduct extensive experiments to validate certain design choices of the model and compare our model with its peers. Results show that the proposed SentiBERT-BiLSTM-CNN demonstrates superior performance in the F1 score, making it a competitive model in Tweets-based disaster prediction.

Keywords: natural language processing; text classification; mining information; Tweet data; social media

Citation: Song, G.; Huang, D. A Sentiment-Aware Contextual Model for Real-Time Disaster Prediction Using Twitter Data. *Future Internet* **2021**, *13*, 163. https://doi.org/10.3390/fi13070163

Academic Editors: Massimo Esposito, Giovanni Luca Masala, Aniello Minutolo and Marco Pota

Received: 21 May 2021
Accepted: 21 June 2021
Published: 25 June 2021

1. Introduction

Social media has been increasingly popular for people to share instant feelings, emotions, opinions, stories, and so on. As a leading social platform, Twitter has gained tremendous popularity since its inception. The latest statistical data show that over 500 million Tweets are sent each day, generating a massive amount of social data that are used by numerous upper-level analytical applications to create additional value. Meanwhile, numerous studies have adopted Twitter data to build natural language processing (NLP) applications such as named entity recognition (NER) [1], relation extraction [2], question and answering (Q&A) [3], sentiment analysis [4], and topic modeling [5].

In addition to the social function, Twitter is also becoming a real-time platform to track events, including accidents, disasters, and emergencies, especially in the era of mobile Internet and 5G communication, where smartphones allow people to post an emergency Tweet instantly online. Timing is the most critical factor in making a rescue plan, and the rise in social media brings a unique opportunity to expedite this process. Due to this convenience, more agencies like disaster relief organizations and news agencies are deploying resources to programmatically monitor Twitter, so that first responders can be dispatched and rescue plans can be made at the earliest time. However, processing social media data and retrieving valuable information for disaster prediction requires a series of operations: (1) perform text classification on each Tweet to predict disasters and emergencies; (2) determine the location of people who need help; (3) calculate the priorities to schedule rescues. Disaster prediction is the first and most important step, because a misclassification may result in a waste of precious resources which could have been dispatched to real needs [6].

However, to automate this process, an accurate and robust classifier is needed to distinguish real disaster Tweets from regular ones. Disaster prediction based on Tweets is challenging, because words indicative of a disaster, such as "fire", "flood", and "collapse", can be used by people metaphorically to describe something else. For example, a Tweet message "On plus side look at the sky last night it was ABLAZE" explicitly uses the word "ABLAZE" but means it metaphorically. The length limit of Tweets brings pros and cons for training a classifier. The benefit is that users are forced to tell a story in a concise way, and the downside is that the lack of clear context may prevent a classifier from well understanding and interpreting the real meaning of a Tweet. Therefore, it is crucial to build an advanced model that can understand the subtle sentiment embedded in Tweets along with their given contexts to make better predictions.

Recent advances in deep learning have explored approaches to address these challenges that are commonly seen in other NLP tasks. Convolutional neural networks (CNNs), which have been widely used in numerous computer vision tasks, have also been successfully applied in NLP systems due to their ability for feature extraction and representation. Recurrent neural networks and their popular variants, Long Short-Term Memory (LSTM) and Gated Recurrent Unit (GRU), are not only suitable for general sequential modeling tasks but also provide the capability to capture long dependency information between words in a sentence. In addition, LSTM and GRU can well address the gradient explosion and vanishing issue and allow a training algorithm to converge. Another breakthrough architecture is Bidirectional Encoder Representations from Transformers (BERT), which stacks layers of Transformer encoders with a multi-headed attention mechanism to enhance a model's ability to capture contextual information.

Inspired by these prior efforts, we propose a learning pipeline named SentiBERT-BiLSTM-CNN for disaster prediction based on Tweets. As shown in Figure 1, the pipeline consists of three consecutive modules, including (1) a SentiBERT-based encoder that aims to transform input tokens to sentiment-aware contextual embeddings, (2) a Bidirectional LSTM (BiLSTM) layer with attention to produce attentive hidden states, and (3) a single-layer CNN as a feature extractor. In addition, a standard detection head takes as input a concatenation of the generated features and feeds them into a fully connected layer followed by a softmax layer to output the prediction result, i.e., disaster Tweet or not. The design is validated through extensive experiments, including hyper-parameter tuning to decide certain design choices and an ablation study to justify the necessity of each selected building block. Results show that the proposed system achieves superior performance in the F1 score, making it a competitive model in Tweets-based disaster prediction.

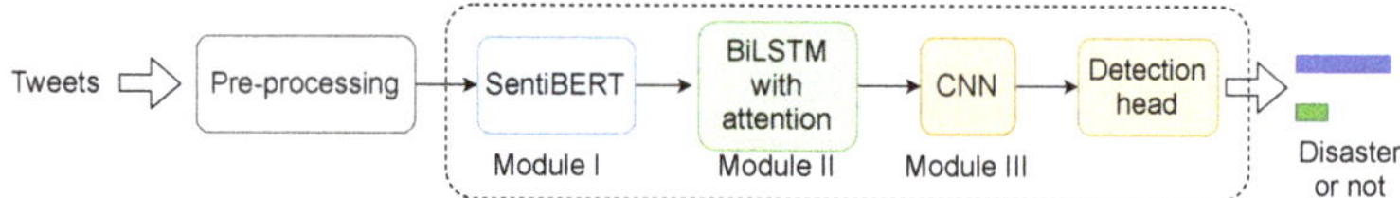

Figure 1. The proposed SentiBERT-BiLSTM-CNN learning pipeline for disaster prediction using Tweets.

The rest of this paper is organized as follows: Section 2 reviews relevant studies; Section 3 covers the dataset description and the technical details of the proposed learning model; Section 4 provides experimental validation with result analysis; Section 5 summarizes our work and points out future directions.

2. Related Work

2.1. Social Media Learning Tasks

Data collected from social media have a lot of potentials to explore. Social texts have been extensively studied and mined to build a wide range of NLP applications such as NER [1], Q&A [3], sentiment analysis [4,7–10], and topic modeling [5,11,12]. In addition, social data have been utilized for emergency, disease, and disaster analysis [13–15]. In [16], the authors develop predictive models to detect Tweets that present situational awareness. The models are evaluated in four real-world datasets, including the Red River floods of 2009 and 2010, the Haiti earthquake of 2010, and the Oklahoma fires of 2009. This paper focuses on exploring the contextual information in Tweets to build a robust disaster classifier.

2.2. *RNN/CNN-Based Models in Text Mining*

Active development in deep learning in recent years has generated fruitful achievements in social text learning. As two representative learning models, RNN and CNN have been seen in numerous studies, either individually or in a hybrid fashion.

Huang et al. [17] combined BiLSTM and Conditional Random Field (CRF) to build a sequential tagging framework that can be applied to parts of speech (POS), chunking, and NER tasks. In [18], Liu et al. propose a Stochastic Answer Network (SAN) that stacks various layer types, including GRU, BiLSTM, and self-attention; along with a stochastic prediction dropout trick, the SAN model shows superior performance in reading comprehension.

Kalchbrenner et al. [19] designed one of the earliest CNN-based methods for sentence modeling, which featured a dynamic CNN (DCNN) that uses the dynamic k-max pooling subsampling and achieves superior performance in sentiment classification. Due to CNN's ability in feature extraction, the DCNN-based system does not require hand-crafted features, which is appreciated and widely adopted by numerous subsequent studies. Kim [4] proposed a simple but effective CNN architecture that utilizes pre-trained word embeddings by word2vec. Kim's work was modified by Liu et al. [20], who propose to learn word embeddings rather than use pre-trained ones directly. Mou et al. designed a tree-based CNN [21] that can capture the general semantics of sentences. In [22], Pang et al. proposed to transform the text matching problem into an image recognition task that can be solved by a CNN-based model. In addition to open-domain datasets, CNNs have also been extensively used in domain-specific tasks, especially in biomedical text classification [22–27].

Chen et al. [18] proposed a two-stage method that combines BiLSTM and CNN for sentiment classification. First, the BiLSTM model is used for sentence type classification. Once assigned a type, a sentence then goes through a 1D CNN layer for sentiment detection. In [28], the authors designed a hybrid network that combines RNN, MLP, and CNN to explore semantic information at each hierarchical level of a document.

2.3. *Transformer-Based Models for Social Text Learning*

BERT [29] and its variants [30–36] have been extensively used as building blocks for numerous applications, owing to their ability to capture contextual word embeddings. FakeBERT [37] combines BERT and 1D CNN layers to detect fake news in social media. A similar work [38] adopts BERT to detect auto-generated tweets. Mozafari et al. [39] designed a BERT-based transfer learning method to detect hate speech on Twitter. Eke et al. [40] employed BERT to build a sarcasm detector that can classify sarcastic utterances, which is crucial for downstream tasks like sentiment analysis and opinion mining.

2.4. *Learning-Based Disaster Tweets Detection*

One of the early efforts to identify and classify disaster Tweets is by Stowe et al. [6], who focused on the Tweets generated when Hurricane Sandy hit New York in 2012. In [6], six fine-grained categories of Tweets, including Reporting, Sentiment, Information, Action, Preparation, and Movement, are annotated. With a series of hand-crafted features, such as key terms, Bigrams, time, and URLs, the dataset is used to train three feature-based models, including SVM, maximum entropy, and Naive Bayes models. Palshikar et al. [41] developed a weakly-supervised model based on a bag of words, combined with an online algorithm that helps learn the weights of words to boost detection performance. Algur et al. [42] first transformed Tweets into vectors using count vectorization and Term Frequency-Inverse Document Frequency (TF-IDF), based on a set of pre-identified disaster keywords; the vectorized Tweets are then trained using Naive Bayes, Logistic Regression, J48, Random Forest, and SVM to obtain various classifiers. Singh et al. [43] investigated a Markov model-based model to predict the priority and location of Tweets during a disaster. Madichetty et al. [44] designed a neural architecture that consists of a CNN to extract features from Tweets and a multilayer perceptron (MLP) to perform classification. Joao [45] developed a BERT-based hybrid model that uses both hand-crafted features and learned ones for informative Tweets identification. Li et al. [46] investigate a domain-adapted learning task that uses a Naive Bayes classifier, combined with an iterative self-training algorithm, to incorporate annotated data from a source disaster dataset and data without annotation from the target disaster dataset into a classifier for the target disaster. More broadly, prior efforts on event Tweet detection are also of interest. Ansah et al. [47] proposed a model named SensorTree to detect protest events by tracking information propagated through the Twitter user communities and monitoring the sudden change in the growth of these communities as burst for event detection. Saeed et al. [48] developed a Dynamic Heartbeat Graph (DHG) model to detect trending topics from the Twitter stream. An investigation of recent efforts [49] in disaster Tweet detection reveals a lack of deep learning-based methods that have shown superiority in numerous other NLP applications, as mentioned in Section 2.1. However, in the sub-field of disaster Tweets detection, the use cases are still insufficient. In addition, the idea of integrating sentiment information into a disaster detector remains unexplored, and our study is an attempt to fill this gap.

Inspired by the prior efforts, we design a learning pipeline that includes a BERT variant named SentiBERT [50] to obtain sentiment-aware contextual embeddings, a BiLSTM layer for sequential modeling, and a CNN for feature extraction. The pipeline aggregates the strength of each individual block to enhance the predictive power that realizes an accurate disaster detector.

3. Material and Methods

3.1. Dataset

The dataset was created by Figure Eight inc. (an Appen company) from Twitter data and used as a Kaggle competition hosted at https://www.kaggle.com/c/nlp-getting-started/data (accessed on 21 June 2021). There are 10,876 samples in the dataset, including 4692 positive samples (disaster) and 6184 negative samples (not a disaster). Table 1 shows four positive and four negative samples. It can be seen that the disaster and non-disaster Tweets could use similar keywords in different contexts, resulting in different interpretations. For example, "pileup" in sample 1, "airplane's accident" in sample 2, "Horno blaze" in sample 3, and the phrase "a sign of the apocalypse" in sample 4 are more indicative of a disaster. However, the words "bleeding", "blaze", "ambulance", and "Apocalypse" in samples 4 through 8 do not indicate a disaster, given their contexts. Figure 2 displays the histograms of three variables per Tweet: the number of characters, the number of words, and the average number of word lengths. Specifically, the means of the character number per Tweet for disaster and non-disaster Tweets are 108.11 and 95, respectively; the means of the word number per Tweet for disaster and non-disaster Tweets are 15.16 and 14.7, respectively; the means of the average word length for disaster and non-disaster Tweets are 5.92 and 5.14, respectively. The stats data show that the disaster Tweets are relatively longer than the non-disaster ones.

Table 1. Disaster Tweets dataset samples. A + sign indicates a positive sample, and a − sign indicates a negative sample.

ID	Sample Tweet	Class
1	Grego saw that pileup on TV keep racing even bleeding.	+
2	Family members who killed in an airplane's accident.	+
3	Pendleton media office said only fire on base right now is the Horno blaze.	+
4	I know it's a question of interpretation but this is a sign of the apocalypse.	+
5	bleeding on the brain don't know the cause.	−
6	alrighty Hit me up and we'll blaze!!	−
7	waiting for an ambulance.	−
8	Apocalypse please.	−

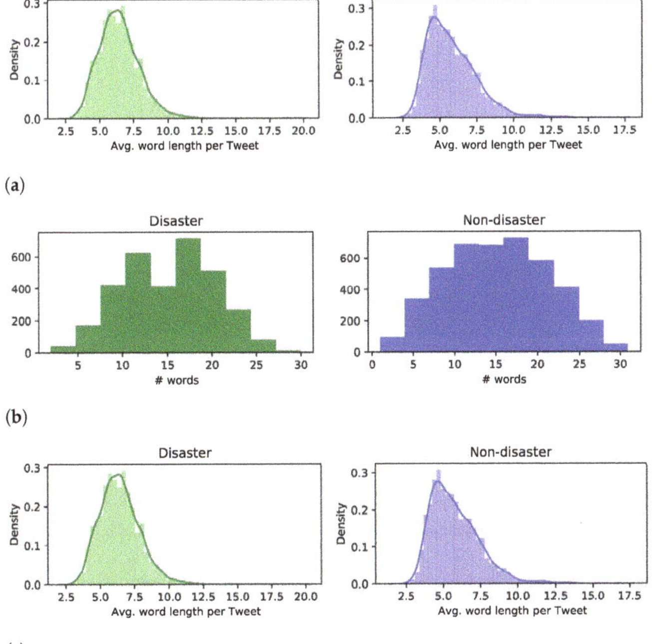

Figure 2. Stats of Tweets in the dataset. Histograms of (**a**) the number of characters per Tweet, (**b**) the number of words per Tweet, and (**c**) the average word length per Tweet, plotted for disaster Tweets (**left**) and non-disaster Tweets (**right**).

3.2. Data Pre-Processing

The raw data obtained from Twitter have noises that need to be cleaned. Thus, we apply a pre-processing step to remove the hashtags, emoticons, and punctuation marks. For example, a message "# it's cool. :)", becomes "it's cool." after the filtering. We then apply some basic transformations such as changing "We've" to "We have" to create a better word separation within a sentence. Finally, we tokenize each message to generate a word sequence as the input of the learning pipeline.

3.3. Overview of the Proposed Learning Pipeline

Figure 3 shows the proposed SentiBERT-BiLSTM-CNN learning pipeline, which consists of three sequential modules:

1. SentiBERT is utilized to transform word tokens from the raw Tweet messages to contextual word embeddings. Compared to BERT, SentiBERT is better at understanding and encoding sentiment information.
2. BiLSTM is adopted to capture the order information as well as the long-dependency relation in a word sequence.
3. CNN acts as a feature extractor that strives to mine textual patterns from the embeddings generated by the BiLSTM module.

The output of the CNN is fed to a detection layer to generate the final prediction result, i.e., disaster or not.

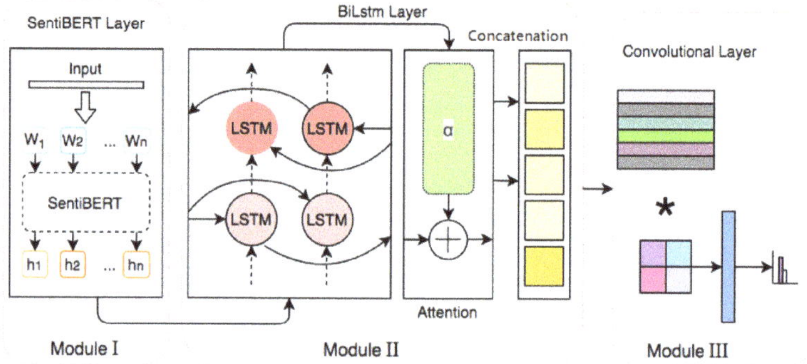

Figure 3. An overview of the SentiBERT-BiLSTM-CNN learning pipeline.

3.4. Sentibert

BERT [29] is an attention-based language model that utilizes a stack of Transformer encoders and decoders to learn textual information. It also uses a multi-headed attention mechanism to extract useful features for the task. The bidirectional Transformer neural network, as the encoder of BERT, converts each word token into a numeric vector to form a word embedding, so that words that are semantically related would be translated to embeddings that are numerically close. BERT also employs a mask language model (MLM) technique and a next sentence prediction (NSP) task in training to capture word-level and sentence-level contextual information. BERT and its variants have been applied to numerous NLP tasks such as named entity recognition, relation extraction, machine translation, and question and answering, and achieved the state-of-the-art performance. In this study, we choose a BERT variant, SentiBERT, which is a transferable transformer-based architecture dedicated to the understanding of sentiment semantics. As shown in Figure 4, SentiBERT modifies BERT by adding a semantic composition unit and a phrase node prediction unit. Specifically, the semantic composition unit aims to obtain phrase representations that are guided by contextual word embeddings and an attentive constituency parsing tree. Phrase-level sentiment labels are used for phrase node prediction. Due to the addition of phrase-level sentiment detection, a sentence can be broken down and analyzed at a finer granularity to capture more sentiment semantics.

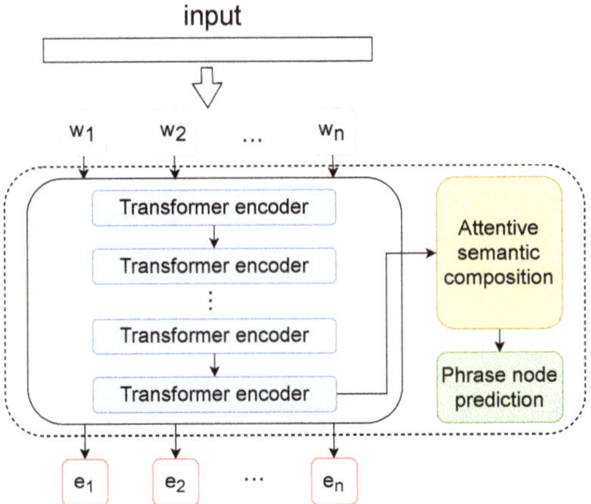

Figure 4. Module I: SentiBERT.

Let $\mathbf{s} = \{w_i|i = 1, ..., n\}$ denote a Tweet message with n word tokens, which are the input of SentiBERT. Our goal is to leverage the power of SentiBERT to generate sentiment-enhanced word embeddings, which can be denoted by $\mathbf{e} = \{e_i = \text{SentiBERT}(w_i)|i = 1, ..., n\}$. In this study, each Tweet should have no more than 64 tokens; the Tweets with less than 64 tokens are padded, namely, $n = 64$. Reference [29] experimentally showed that the output of the last four hidden layers of BERT encodes more contextual information than that of the previous layers. To this end, we also chose a concatenation of the outputs of the last four hidden layers as the word embedding representation.

3.5. Bilstm with Attention

A regular LSTM unit consists of a cell, an input gate, an output gate and a forget gate. The cell can memorize values over arbitrary time periods, and the three gates regulate information flow into and out of the cell to keep what matters and forget what does not. The BiLSTM consists of a forward and a backward LSTM that process an input token vector from both directions. By looking at past and future words, a BiLSTM network can potentially capture the more semantic meaning of a sentence. In our study, the word embeddings $\mathbf{e}$ produced from module I are fed into a standard BiLSTM layer to generate a list of hidden states $\mathbf{h} = \{h_i|i = 1, ..., n\}$, where h_i is given by Equation set (1).

$$\begin{aligned} \overleftarrow{h_i} &= \overleftarrow{\text{LSTM}}(e_i, \overleftarrow{h_{i-1}}) \\ \overrightarrow{h_i} &= \overrightarrow{\text{LSTM}}(e_i, \overrightarrow{h_{i-1}}) \\ h_i &= [\overleftarrow{h_i}; \overrightarrow{h_i}] \end{aligned} \tag{1}$$

where $[;]$ is a concatenation operation. The structure is shown in Figure 5.

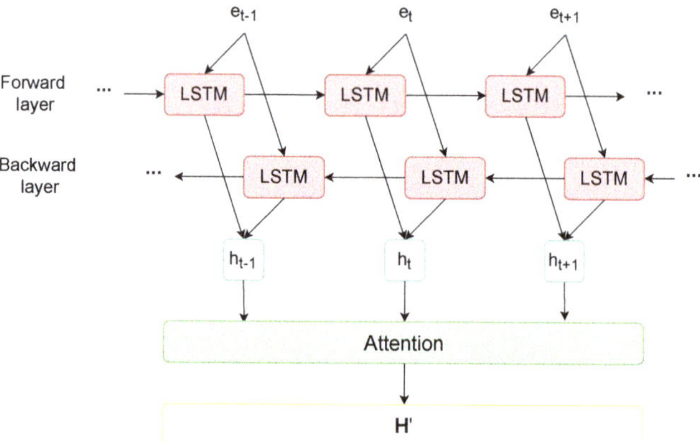

Figure 5. Module II: BiLSTM with attention.

In a Tweet, each word influences the disaster polarity differently. Using an attention mechanism can help the model learn to assign different weights to different words so that the more influential words are given higher weights. For a hidden state h_i, its attention a_i is given in the Equation set (2).

$$
\begin{aligned}
u_i &= \tanh(W \cdot h_i + b) \\
a_i &= \frac{e^{u_i^\top \cdot u_w}}{\sum_i e^{u_i^\top \cdot u_w}},
\end{aligned}
\tag{2}
$$

where W denotes a weight matrix, b denotes the bias, and u_w a global context vector, and all three are learned during training. The output of module II is a concatenation of attentive hidden states $\mathbf{H}' = [a_1 h_1; ...; a_n h_n]$.

3.6. CNN

Module III is a CNN that extracts local features, as shown in Figure 6. We adopt a 1D convolutional layer with four differently-sized filters. Each filter scans the input matrix $\mathbf{H}'$ and performs a 1D convolutional along the way to generate a feature map. The extracted features are then fed into a max-pooling layer and concatenated to form a feature matrix $\mathbf{F}$. Lastly, we send a concatenation of $\mathbf{H}'$ and $\mathbf{F}$ to the dense layer.

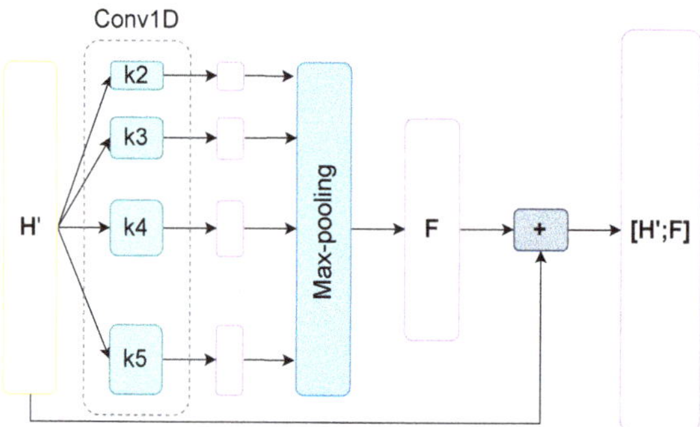

Figure 6. Module III: feature extraction via a CNN layer.

3.7. A Fusion of Loss Functions

In this subsection, we explore the options of loss functions. We considered two individual loss functions including the binary cross-entropy (BCE) loss and the Focal Loss. In addition, we employed a fusion strategy as suggested in [51] to combine the two losses, which resulted in performance improvement.

Since the disaster Tweet detection task is a typical binary classification problem, it is intuitive to utilize the BCE loss as shown in Equation (3) below.

$$L_{BCE} = -\frac{1}{m}\sum_{i=1}^{m}(y_{(i)}log(\hat{y}_{(i)}) + (1 - y_{(i)})log(1 - \hat{y}_{(i)})), \tag{3}$$

in which m is the training set size, and $y_{(i)}$ and $\hat{y}_{(i)}$ denote the ground truth and the predicted class for the ith sample in the dataset, respectively.

Meanwhile, considering the imbalanced sample distribution, this study also employs Focal Loss, defined in Equation (4).

$$L_{FL} = -\frac{1}{m}\sum_{i=1}^{m}(y_{(i)}\alpha(1 - \hat{y}_{(i)})^{\gamma} + (1 - y_{(i)})(1 - \alpha)\hat{y}_{(i)}^{\gamma}log(1 - \hat{y}_{i})), \tag{4}$$

where γ is a coefficient that controls the curve shape of the focal loss function. Using Focal Loss with $\gamma > 1$ reduces the loss for well-classified examples (i.e., with a prediction probability larger than 0.5) and increases loss for hard-to-classify examples (i.e., with a prediction probability less than 0.5). Therefore, it turns the model's attention towards the rare class in case of class imbalance. On the other hand, a lower α value means that we tend to give a small weight to the dominating or common class and high weight to the rare class. By fusing the focal loss and the BCE loss in a certain ratio, we obtain Equation (5), in which β_1 and β_2 specify the fusion weights.

$$L_{mix} = \beta_1 L_{BCE} + \beta_2 L_{FL} \tag{5}$$

4. Experiments

We utilize the disaster Tweet dataset discussed in Section 3.1 for performance evaluation. We first present the performance metrics and then report the experimental results.

4.1. Evaluation Metrics

We use precision (Pre), recall (Rec), and the F1 score to evaluate the model performance. Given that the positive/negative samples are not balanced, F1 is a better metric than accuracy. Precision and recall are also important. The former reflects the number of false alarms; the higher the precision, the fewer false alarms. The latter tells the number of positive samples that are missed; the higher the recall, the fewer disaster Tweets missed. A large precision–recall gap should be avoided, since it indicates that a model focuses on a single metric, while a model should really focus on optimizing F1, the harmonic mean of precision and recall.

Let TP, TN, and FP denote the number of true positives, true negatives, and false positives, respectively, we can then calculate precision, recall, and F1 as follows.

$$Pre = \frac{TP}{TP + FP} \tag{6}$$

$$Rec = \frac{TP}{TP + FN} \tag{7}$$

$$F1 = 2 \times \frac{Pre \times Rec}{Pre + Rec}. \tag{8}$$

4.2. Training Setting

The dataset was divided into training and validation sets in the ratio of 7:3, generating 7613 training and 3263 validation samples. For the SentiBERT, the embedding dimension was 768, max sequence length was 128, and layer number was 12; for the BiLSTM module, the layer number was 1, and the feature number was 768; for the CNN module, the sizes of the four filters were set to 2, 3, 4 and 5. For the overall architecture, we used a learning rate of 1×10^{-4}, the Adam optimizer, and experimented with different batch sizes (16 and 32) and training epochs (6, 8, 10, 12, and 14). All experiments were implemented using Python 3.9.4 and PyTorch 1.8.0 on Google Colab with an NVIDIA Tesla K80.

4.3. Baseline Model

The baseline model we chose was a BERT-based hybrid model developed by Joao [45]. We denote the model as BERT_{hyb}. We regard BERT_{hyb} as a credible baseline because it presented the state-of-the-art (SOTA) performance compared to a variety of models on four datasets. BERT_{hyb} works by combining a series of hand-crafted Tweet features and the BERT word embeddings and sending the feature concatenation to an MLP for classification.

4.4. Effect of Hyper-Parameter Choices

We conducted experiments to evaluate the performance of our model SentiBERT-BiLSTM-CNN under different hyper-parameter settings. Specifically, the model was trained with a combination of three values of epochs (6, 8, 10, 12, and 14) and two values of batch sizes (16, 32), creating ten experiments, as shown in Table 2. It can be seen that when the model was trained with 10 epochs and with a batch size of 32, the model achieved the best performance, with an F1 of 0.8956. We also observe a consistent performance improvement as the number of epochs increases from 6 to 10, and beyond 10 epochs, the gain is not apparent. The training was efficient because SentiBERT has been pre-trained and was only fine-tuned on our dataset. It is noted that for this set of experiments, we applied a basic cross-entropy loss function. The effect of the fused loss function is reported in the next subsection.

Table 2. Performance of SentiBERT-BiLSTM-CNN under different hyper-parameter settings.

Epochs	Batch Size	Precision	Recall	F1 Score
6	32	0.8525	0.8478	0.8501
	16	0.8495	0.8364	0.8429
8	32	0.8654	0.8701	0.8677
	16	0.8643	0.8618	0.8630
10	32	**0.8987**	0.8932	**0.8959**
	16	0.8903	0.8827	0.8865
12	32	0.8848	0.8956	0.8902
	16	0.8817	0.8893	0.8855
14	32	0.8902	**0.9012**	0.8957
	16	0.8949	0.8878	0.8913

4.5. The Effect of a Hybrid Loss Function

We conducted experiments to evaluate the model's performance under different loss function settings. We first evaluated the performance of using BCE and FL individually and then fused the two loss functions in the ratio of 1:1. The results are reported in Table 3. We observe that the model with FL outperformed the model with BCE, validating the efficacy of FL in the case of imbalanced data distribution. In addition, the model with a hybrid loss function performed the best, with an F1 of 0.9275. The result demonstrates the effectiveness of the fusion strategy in this study.

Table 3. Performance of SentiBERT-BiLSTM-CNN under different loss function settings.

Loss Function	Epochs	Batch Size	Precision	Recall	F1 Score
L_{BCE}	10	32	0.8987	0.8932	0.8959
L_{FL}	10	32	0.9029	0.9135	0.9082
L_{mix}	10	32	**0.9305**	**0.9271**	**0.9275**

4.6. Performance Evaluation

We also conducted experiments to evaluate a set of models, and present a performance comparison of all evaluated models in Table 4, using the best hyper-parameter settings and the fused loss function, as reported in the previous two subsections. We give the result analysis as follows.

- The set of models CNN, BiLSTM, SentiBERT, BiLSTM-CNN, and SentiBERT-BiLSTM-CNN forms an ablation study, from which we can evaluate the performance of each individual module and the combined versions. It can be seen that the pure CNN model performs the worst since a single-layer CNN cannot learn any contextual information. Both BiLSTM (with attention) and SentiBERT present an obvious improvement. SentiBERT is on a par with BiLSTM-CNN in precision, but outperforms it in recall. Our final model, SentiBERT-BiLSTM-CNN tops every other model, showing its power to combine the strength of each individual building block.
- The set of models fastText-BiLSTM-CNN, word2vec-BiLSTM-CNN, BERT-BiLSTM-CNN, and SentiBERT-BiLSTM-CNN are evaluated to compare the effect of word embeddings. FastText [52], word2vec [53], BERT, and SentiBERT are used for the same purpose, i.e., to generate word embeddings. A model's ability to preserve contextual information determines its performance. From the results, we observe that by adding contextual embeddings, the models gain improvements to varying degrees. SentiBERT-BiLSTM-CNN, as the best-performing model, demonstrates superior capability in encoding contextual information.
- Another observation is that SentiBERT-BiLSTM-CNN outperforms BERT-BiLSTM-CNN by 1.23% in F1, meaning that sentiment in Tweets is a crucial factor that can help detect disaster Tweets, and a sentiment-enhanced BERT validates this hypothesis.
- Lastly, SentiBERT-BiLSTM-CNN outperforms BERT_{hyb}, i.e., the SOTA, by 0.77% in F1. Although BERT_{hyb} presented the highest precision 0.9413, its precision–recall gap (4.21%) is large, compared to that of SentiBERT-BiLSTM-CNN (0.34%), meaning that BERT_{hyb} focuses more on optimizing precision. On the other hand, SentiBERT-BiLSTM-CNN demonstrated a more balanced result in precision and recall.

Table 4. A performance comparison of models.

Model	Precision	Recall	F1 Score
CNN	0.8064	0.8086	0.8025
BiLSTM	0.8571	0.8405	0.8487
SentiBERT	0.8668	0.8712	0.8690
BiLSTM-CNN	0.8674	0.8523	0.8598
word2vec-BiLSTM-CNN	0.8831	0.8767	0.8799
fastText-BiLSTM-CNN	0.8935	0.8736	0.8834
BERT-BiLSTM-CNN	0.9118	0.9187	0.9152
BERT_{hyb}	**0.9413**	0.8992	0.9198
SentiBERT-BiLSTM-CNN	0.9305	**0.9271**	**0.9275**

4.7. Error Analysis

Table 5 shows ten samples, including five positive and five negative ones, which are misclassified by the proposed SentiBERT-BiLSTM-CNN model. In this subsection, we provide an analysis of these mistakes that may shed light on further improvement of our model.

- For the five samples that are marked as disaster Tweets (i.e., samples one through five), none of them are describing a common sense disaster: sample 1 seems to state a personal accident; sample 2 talks about US dollar crisis which may indicate inflation given its context; in sample 3, the phrase "batting collapse" refers to a significant failure of the batting team in a sports game; sample 4 is the closest to a real disaster, but the word "simulate" simply reverses the semantic meaning; sample 5 does mention a disaster "Catastrophic Man-Made Global Warming", but the user simply expresses his/her opinion against it. Our observation is that the process of manual annotation could introduce some noises that would affect the modeling training. From another perspective, the noises help build more robust classifiers and potentially reduce overfitting.
- For the five negative samples (6–10), we also observe possible cases of mislabeled samples: sample 6 clearly reports a fire accident with the phrase "burning buildings" but was not labeled as a disaster Tweet; sample 7 states a serious traffic accident; sample 8 mentions bio-disaster with the phrase "infectious diseases and bioterrorism"; sample 9 has only three words, and it is hard to tell its class without more context, although the word "bombed" is in the Tweet; sample 10 reflects a person's suicide intent, which could have been marked as a positive case.

Table 5. Examples of misclassified samples. A "+" sign indicates a positive sample, and a "−" sign indicates a negative sample.

ID	Sample Tweet	Label	Prediction
1	I was wrong to call it trusty actually. considering it spontaneously collapsed on me that's not very trusty.	+	−
2	Prices here are insane. Our dollar has collapsed against the US and it's punishing us. Thanks for the info.	+	−
3	Now that's what you call a batting collapse.	+	−
4	Emergency units simulate a chemical explosion at NU.	+	−
5	99% of Scientists don't believe in Catastrophic Man-Made Global Warming only the deluded do.	+	−
6	all illuminated by the brightly burning buildings all around the town!	−	+
7	That or they might be killed in an airplane accident in the night a car wreck! Politics at it's best.	−	+
8	automation in the fight against infectious diseases and bioterrorism	−	+
9	misfit got bombed.	−	+
10	Because I need to know if I'm supposed to throw myself off a bridge for a #Collapse or plan the parade. There is no both.	−	+

We need to clarify that these misclassified samples presented in the table are randomly selected from all error predictions. It can be seen that the length limit of Tweets presents pros and cons for training a classifier. The bright side is that users are forced to use short and direct words to express an opinion, and the downside is that some short Tweets are hard to interpret due to the lack of more context information, which is the main challenge for training an accurate model.

5. Conclusions

Disaster analysis is highly related to people's daily lives, and recent years have seen more research efforts dedicating to this field. Research on disaster prediction helps augment people's awareness, improve the mechanism of a government rescue, and schedule charitable institutions' work. This paper investigates a novel model for disaster detection using Tweets. Our model, SentiBERT-BiLSTM-CNN, leverages a sentiment-aware BERT encoder, an attentive BiLSTM, and a 1D convolutional layer to extract high-quality linguistic features for disaster prediction. The model is validated through extensive experiments compared to its peers, making it a competitive model for building a real-time disaster detector.

Although the proposed model is trained and validated on an English dataset, it can be applied to datasets in other languages. Specifically, in a different language environment, the following adjustments need to be made: first, we should find a BERT model pre-trained in the target language or in a multi-lingual setting, which is readily available online (https://huggingface.co/transformers/pretrained_models.html, accessed on 12 March 2021); second, we need to retrain SentiBERT on a sentiment analysis dataset in the target language; lastly, a new disaster Tweet dataset in the target language is needed to train and validate the model. In this new language environment, SentiBERT can now generate sentiment-aware word embeddings to be consumed by the subsequent BiLSTM and CNN modules, which are language independent.

This work has the following limitations that also point out the future directions. First, it remains interesting to uncover the role keywords played in disaster detection. Given that keywords like "blaze" and "apocalypse" can appear in both disaster and non-disaster Tweets, it is challenging to effectively utilize the keywords as extra knowledge to help boost the detection accuracy. One potential solution is to fine-tune BERT through pair-wise training, taking a pair of Tweets containing the same keywords but with opposite training labels; this way, BERT is forced to better understand the contextual difference between two Tweets. Second, it remains unknown that how well the model trained on our dataset performs on other disaster datasets, such as HumAID [54] and Crisismmd [55]; in addition, we expect to obtain a more robust model that is trained across multiple disaster/crisis Tweets datasets. Third, we are interested in creating a multilingual disaster detector that can understand and process Tweets in different languages; it is worth conducting a performance comparison between a multilingual and a monolingual model.

Author Contributions: Conceptualization and methodology, G.S. and D.H.; software, validation, and original draft preparation, G.S.; review and editing, supervision, funding acquisition, D.H. All authors have read and agreed to the published version of the manuscript.

Funding: This work is supported by the National Key Research and Development Program of China (2020AAA0108004) and the National Natural Science Foundation of China (61672127, U1936109). The funding agency has no role in study design, data collection and analysis, decision to publish, or preparation of the manuscript.

Institutional Review Board Statement: Not applicable.

Informed Consent Statement: Not applicable.

Data Availability Statement: Data Availability Statement: Natural Language Processing with Disaster Tweets dataset supporting the conclusions of this article are available at https://www.kaggle.com/c/nlp-getting-started/data (accessed on 20 March 2021).

Conflicts of Interest: The authors declare no conflict of interest.

References

1. Li, C.; Weng, J.; He, Q.; Yao, Y.; Datta, A.; Sun, A.; Lee, B.S. Twiner: Named entity recognition in targeted twitter stream. In Proceedings of the 35th international ACM SIGIR Conference on Research and Development in Information Retrieval, Portland, OR, USA, 12–16 August 2012; pp. 721–730.
2. Ritter, A.; Wright, E.; Casey, W.; Mitchell, T. Weakly supervised extraction of computer security events from twitter. In Proceedings of the 24th International Conference on World Wide Web, Florence, Italy, 18–22 May 2015; pp. 896–905.

3. Soulier, L.; Tamine, L.; Nguyen, G.H. Answering twitter questions: A model for recommending answerers through social collaboration. In Proceedings of the 25th ACM International on Conference on Information and Knowledge Management, Indianapolis, IN, USA, 24–28 October 2016; pp. 267–276.
4. Kim, Y. Convolutional Neural Networks for Sentence Classification. In *Proceedings of the 2014 Conference on Empirical Methods in Natural Language Processing (EMNLP)*; Association for Computational Linguistics: Doha, Qatar, 2014; pp. 1746–1751.
5. Steinskog, A.; Therkelsen, J.; Gambäck, B. Twitter topic modeling by tweet aggregation. In Proceedings of the 21st Nordic Conference on Computational Linguistics, Gothenburg, Sweden, 22–24 May 2017; pp. 77–86.
6. Stowe, K.; Paul, M.; Palmer, M.; Palen, L.; Anderson, K.M. November. Identifying and categorizing disaster-related tweets. In Proceedings of the Fourth International Workshop on Natural Language Processing for Social Media, Austin, TX, USA, 1 November 2016; pp. 1–6.
7. Bakshi, R.K.; Kaur, N.; Kaur, R.; Kaur, G. Opinion mining and sentiment analysis. In Proceedings of the 2016 3rd International Conference on Computing for Sustainable Global Development (INDIACom), New Delhi, India, 16–18 March 2016; pp. 452–455.
8. Go, A.; Bhayani, R.; Huang, L. Twitter sentiment classification using distant supervision. CS224N project report. *Stanford* **2009**, *1*, 2009.
9. Kouloumpis, E.; Wilson, T.; Moore, J. Twitter sentiment analysis: The good the bad and the omg! In Proceedings of the International AAAI Conference on Web and Social Media, Catalonia, Spain, 17–21 July 2011; Volume 5.
10. Hao, Y.; Mu, T.; Hong, R.; Wang, M.; Liu, X.; Goulermas, J.Y. Cross-domain sentiment encoding through stochastic word embedding. *IEEE Trans. Knowl. Data Eng.* **2019**, *32*, 1909–1922. [CrossRef]
11. Sankaranarayanan, J.; Samet, H.; Teitler, B.E.; Lieberman, M.D.; Sperling, J. Twitterstand: News in tweets. In Proceedings of the 17th ACM Sigspatial International Conference on Advances in Geographic Information Systems, Seattle, WA, USA, 4–6 November 2009; pp. 42–51.
12. Sriram, B.; Fuhry, D.; Demir, E.; Ferhatosmanoglu, H.; Demirbas, M. Short text classification in twitter to improve information filtering. In Proceedings of the 33rd international ACM SIGIR Conference on Research and Development in Information Retrieval, Geneva, Switzerland, 19–23 July 2010; pp. 841–842.
13. Yin, J.; Lampert, A.; Cameron, M.; Robinson, B.; Power, R. Using social media to enhance emergency situation awareness. *IEEE Ann. Hist. Comput.* **2012**, *27*, 52–59. [CrossRef]
14. Kogan, M.; Palen, L.; Anderson, K.M. Think local, retweet global: Retweeting by the geographically-vulnerable during Hurricane Sandy. In Proceedings of the 18th ACM Conference on Computer Supported Cooperative Work and Social Computing, Vancouver, BC, Canada, 14–18 March 2015; pp. 981–993.
15. Lamb, A.; Paul, M.; Dredze, M. Separating fact from fear: Tracking flu infections on twitter. In Proceedings of the 2013 Conference of the North American Chapter of the Association for Computational Linguistics: Human Language Technologies, Atlanta, GA, USA, 9–14 June 2013; pp. 789–795.
16. Verma, S.; Vieweg, S.; Corvey, W.; Palen, L.; Martin, J.; Palmer, M.; Schram, A.; Anderson, K. Natural language processing to the rescue? extracting "situational awareness" tweets during mass emergency. In Proceedings of the International AAAI Conference on Web and Social Media, Catalonia, Spain, 17–21 July 2011; Volume 5.
17. Huang, Z.; Xu, W.; Yu, K. Bidirectional LSTM-CRF models for sequence tagging. *arXiv* **2015**, arXiv:1508.01991.
18. Chen, T.; Xu, R.; He, Y.; Wang, X. Improving sentiment analysis via sentence type classification using BiLSTM-CRF and CNN. *Expert Syst. Appl.* **2017**, *72*, 221–230. [CrossRef]
19. Kalchbrenner, N.; Grefenstette, E.; Blunsom, P. A convolutional neural network for modelling sentences. *arXiv* **2014**, arXiv:1404.2188.
20. Liu, J.; Chang, W.C.; Wu, Y.; Yang, Y. Deep learning for extreme multi-label text classification. In Proceedings of the 40th International ACM SIGIR Conference on Research and Development in Information Retrieval, Tokyo, Japan, 7–11 August 2017; pp. 115–124.
21. Mou, L.; Men, R.; Li, G.; Xu, Y.; Zhang, L.; Yan, R.; Jin, Z. Natural language inference by tree-based convolution and heuristic matching. *arXiv* **2015**, arXiv:1512.08422.
22. Pang, L.; Lan, Y.; Guo, J.; Xu, J.; Wan, S.; Cheng, X. Text matching as image recognition. In Proceedings of the AAAI Conference on Artificial Intelligence, Phoenix, AZ, USA, 12–17 February 2016; Volume 30.
23. Wang, J.; Wang, Z.; Zhang, D.; Yan, J. Combining Knowledge with Deep Convolutional Neural Networks for Short Text Classification. In Proceedings of the IJCAI, Melbourne, Australia, 19–25 August 2017; Volume 350.
24. Karimi, S.; Dai, X.; Hassanzadeh, H.; Nguyen, A. Automatic diagnosis coding of radiology reports: A comparison of deep learning and conventional classification methods. In Proceedings of the BioNLP 2017, Vancouver, BC, Canada, 4 August 2017; pp. 328–332.
25. Peng, S.; You, R.; Wang, H.; Zhai, C.; Mamitsuka, H.; Zhu, S. DeepMeSH: Deep semantic representation for improving large-scale MeSH indexing. *Bioinformatics* **2016**, *32*, i70–i79. [CrossRef] [PubMed]
26. Rios, A.; Kavuluru, R. Convolutional neural networks for biomedical text classification: application in indexing biomedical articles. In Proceedings of the 6th ACM Conference on Bioinformatics, Computational Biology and Health Informatics, Atlanta, GA, USA, 9–12 September 2015; pp. 258–267.
27. Hughes, M.; Li, I.; Kotoulas, S.; Suzumura, T. Medical text classification using convolutional neural networks. *Stud. Health Technol. Inform.* **2017**, *235*, 246–250. [PubMed]

28. Kowsari, K.; Brown, D.E.; Heidarysafa, M.; Meim, i K.J.; Gerber, M.S.; Barnes, L.E. Hdltex: Hierarchical deep learning for text classification. In Proceedings of the 2017 16th IEEE International Conference on Machine Learning and Applications (ICMLA), Cancun, Mexico, 18–21 December 2017; pp. 364–371.
29. Devlin, J.; Chang, M.W.; Lee, K.; Toutanova, K. Bert: Pre-training of deep bidirectional transformers for language understanding. *arXiv* **2018**, arXiv:1810.04805.
30. Lan, Z.; Chen, M.; Goodman, S.; Gimpel, K.; Sharma, P.; Soricut, R. Albert: A lite bert for self-supervised learning of language representations. *arXiv* **2019**, arXiv:1909.11942.
31. Sanh, V.; Debut, L.; Chaumond, J.; Wolf, T. DistilBERT, a distilled version of BERT: Smaller, faster, cheaper and lighter. *arXiv* **2019**, arXiv:1910.01108.
32. Joshi, M.; Chen, D.; Liu, Y.; Weld, D.S.; Zettlemoyer, L.; Levy, O. Spanbert: Improving pre-training by representing and predicting spans. *Trans. Assoc. Comput. Linguist.* **2020**, *8*, 64–77. [CrossRef]
33. Liu, Y.; Ott, M.; Goyal, N.; Du, J.; Joshi, M.; Chen, D.; Levy, O.; Lewis, M.; Zettlemoyer, L.; Stoyanov, V. Roberta: A robustly optimized bert pretraining approach. *arXiv* **2019**, arXiv:1907.11692.
34. Sun, Y.; Wang, S.; Li, Y.; Feng, S.; Tian, H.; Wu, H.; Wang, H. Ernie 2.0: A continual pre-training framework for language understanding. In Proceedings of the AAAI Conference on Artificial Intelligence, New York, NY, USA, 7–12 February 2020; Volume 34, pp. 8968–8975.
35. Liu, X.; Cheng, H.; He, P.; Chen, W.; Wang, Y.; Poon, H.; Gao, J. Adversarial training for large neural language models. *arXiv* **2020**, arXiv:2004.08994.
36. Graves, A.; Jaitly, N.; Mohamed, A.R. Hybrid speech recognition with deep bidirectional LSTM. In Proceedings of the 2013 IEEE Workshop on Automatic Speech Recognition and Understanding, Olomouc, Czech Republic, 8–12 December 2013; pp. 273–278.
37. Kaliyar, R.K.; Goswami, A.; Narang, P. FakeBERT: Fake news detection in social media with a BERT-based deep learning approach. *Multimed. Tools Appl.* **2021**, *80*, 11765–11788. [CrossRef]
38. Harrag, F.; Debbah, M.; Darwish, K.; Abdelali, A. Bert transformer model for detecting Arabic GPT2 auto-generated tweets. *arXiv* **2021**, arXiv:2101.09345.
39. Mozafari, M.; Farahbakhsh, R.; Crespi, N. A BERT-based transfer learning approach for hate speech detection in online social media. In *International Conference on Complex Networks and Their Applications*; Springer: Cham, Switzerland, 2019; pp. 928–940.
40. Eke, C.I.; Norman, A.A.; Shuib, L. Context-Based Feature Technique for Sarcasm Identification in Benchmark Datasets Using Deep Learning and BERT Model. *IEEE Access* **2021**, *9*, 48501–48518. [CrossRef]
41. Palshikar, G.K.; Apte, M.; P.; ita, D. Weakly supervised and online learning of word models for classification to detect disaster reporting tweets. *Inf. Syst. Front.* **2018**, *20*, 949–959. [CrossRef]
42. Algur, S.P.; Venugopal, S. Classification of Disaster Specific Tweets-A Hybrid Approach. In Proceedings of the 2021 8th International Conference on Computing for Sustainable Global Development (INDIACom), New Delhi, India, 17–19 March 2021; pp. 774–777.
43. Singh, J.P.; Dwivedi, Y.K.; Rana, N.P.; Kumar, A.; Kapoor, K.K. Event classification and location prediction from tweets during disasters. *Ann. Oper. Res.* **2019**, *283*, 737–757. [CrossRef]
44. Madichetty, S.; Sridevi, M. Detecting informative tweets during disaster using deep neural networks. In Proceedings of the 2019 11th International Conference on Communication Systems & Networks (COMSNETS), Bengaluru, India, 7–11 January 2019; pp. 709–713.
45. Joao, R.S. On Informative Tweet Identification For Tracking Mass Events. *arXiv* **2021**, arXiv:2101.05656.
46. Li, H.; Caragea, D.; Caragea, C.; Herndon, N. Disaster response aided by tweet classification with a domain adaptation approach. *J. Contingencies Crisis Manag.* **2018**, *26*, 16–27. [CrossRef]
47. Ansah, J.; Liu, L.; Kang, W.; Liu, J.; Li, J. Leveraging burst in twitter network communities for event detection. *World Wide Web* **2020**, *23*, 2851–2876. [CrossRef]
48. Saeed, Z.; Abbasi, R.A.; Razzak, I. Evesense: What can you sense from twitter? In *European Conference on Information Retrieval*; Springer: Cham, Switzerland, 2020; pp. 491–495.
49. Sani, A.M.; Moeini, A. Real-time Event Detection in Twitter: A Case Study. In Proceedings of the 2020 6th International Conference on Web Research (ICWR), Tehran, Iran, 22–23 April 2020; pp. 48–51.
50. Yin, D.; Meng, T.; Chang, K.W. Sentibert: A transferable transformer-based architecture for compositional sentiment semantics. *arXiv* **2020**, arXiv:2005.04114.
51. Song, G.; Huang, D.; Xiao, Z. A Study of Multilingual Toxic Text Detection Approaches under Imbalanced Sample Distribution. *Information* **2021**, *12*, 205. [CrossRef]
52. Bojanowski, P.; Edouard, G.; Arm, J.; Tomas, M. Enriching word vectors with subword information. *Trans. Assoc. Comput. Linguist.* **2017**, *5*, 135–146. [CrossRef]
53. Mikolov, T.; Chen, K.; Corrado, G.; Dean, J. Efficient estimation of word representations in vector space. *arXiv* **2013**, arXiv:1301.3781.
54. Alam, F.; Qazi, U.; Imran, M.; Ofli, F. HumAID: Human-Annotated Disaster Incidents Data from Twitter with Deep Learning Benchmarks. *arXiv* **2021**, arXiv:2104.03090.
55. Alam, F.; Ofli, F.; Imran, M. Crisismmd: Multimodal twitter datasets from natural disasters. In Proceedings of the International AAAI Conference on Web and Social Media, Stanford, CA, USA, 25–28 June 2018; Volume 12.

future internet

MDPI

Article

Generating Synthetic Training Data for Supervised De-Identification of Electronic Health Records

Claudia Alessandra Libbi [1,2], Jan Trienes [2,3,*], Dolf Trieschnigg [2] and Christin Seifert [1,3]

1 Faculty of EEMCS, University of Twente, PO Box 217, 7500 AE Enschede, The Netherlands; alelib29@gmail.com (C.A.L.); christin.seifert@uni-due.de (C.S.)
2 Nedap Healthcare, 7141 DC Groenlo, The Netherlands; dolf.trieschnigg@nedap.com
3 Institute for Artificial Intelligence in Medicine, University of Duisburg-Essen, 45131 Essen, Germany
* Correspondence: jan.trienes@uni-due.de

Abstract: A major hurdle in the development of natural language processing (NLP) methods for Electronic Health Records (EHRs) is the lack of large, annotated datasets. Privacy concerns prevent the distribution of EHRs, and the annotation of data is known to be costly and cumbersome. Synthetic data presents a promising solution to the privacy concern, if synthetic data has comparable utility to real data and if it preserves the privacy of patients. However, the generation of synthetic text alone is not useful for NLP because of the lack of annotations. In this work, we propose the use of neural language models (LSTM and GPT-2) for generating artificial EHR text jointly with annotations for named-entity recognition. Our experiments show that artificial documents can be used to train a supervised named-entity recognition model for de-identification, which outperforms a state-of-the-art rule-based baseline. Moreover, we show that combining real data with synthetic data improves the recall of the method, without manual annotation effort. We conduct a user study to gain insights on the privacy of artificial text. We highlight privacy risks associated with language models to inform future research on privacy-preserving automated text generation and metrics for evaluating privacy-preservation during text generation.

Keywords: natural language processing; medical records; privacy protection; synthetic text; generative language models; named-entity recognition; natural language generation

Citation: Libbi, C.A.; Trienes, J.; Trieschnigg, D.; Seifert, C. Generating Synthetic Training Data for Supervised De-Identification of electronic health records. *Future Internet* **2021**, *13*, 136. https://doi.org/10.3390/fi13050136

Academic Editor: Marco Pota

Received: 26 April 2021
Accepted: 17 May 2021
Published: 20 May 2021

1. Introduction

Narrative text in electronic health records (EHRs) is a rich resource to advance medical and machine learning research. To make this unstructured information suitable for clinical applications, there is a large demand for natural language processing (NLP) solutions that extract clinically relevant information from the raw text [1]. A major hurdle in the development of NLP models for healthcare is the lack of large, annotated training data. There are two reasons for this. First, privacy concerns prevent sharing of clinical data with other researchers. Second, annotating data is a cumbersome and costly process which is impractical for many organizations, especially at the scale demanded by modern NLP models.

Synthetic data has been proposed as a promising alternative to real data. It addresses the privacy concern simply by not describing real persons [2]. Furthermore, if task-relevant properties of the real data are maintained in the synthetic data, it is also of comparable utility [2]. We envision that researchers use synthetic data to work on shared tasks where real data cannot be shared because of privacy concerns. In addition, even within the bounds of a research institute, real data may have certain access restrictions. Using synthetic data as a surrogate for the real data can help organizations to comply with privacy regulations. Besides addressing the privacy concerns, synthetic data is an effective way to increase the amount of available data without additional costs because of its additive nature [3,4]. Prior work showed exciting results when generating both structured [5] and unstructured medical data [2]. In particular, recent advances in neural language modeling show promising results in generating high-quality and realistic text [6].

However, the generation of synthetic text alone does not make it useful for training of NLP models because of the lack of annotations. In this paper, we propose the use of language models to jointly generate synthetic text and training annotations for named-entity recognition (NER) methods. Our idea is to add in-text annotations to the language model training data in form of special tokens to delimit start/end boundaries of named entities (Figure 1). The source of those in-text annotations can be a (potentially noisy) pre-trained model or manual annotation. By adding the special tokens to the training data, they explicitly become part of the language modeling objective. In that way, language models learn to produce text that is automatically annotated for downstream NER tasks—we refer to them as "structure-aware language models." Below, we will briefly outline our research pipeline; see Figure 2 for an overview.

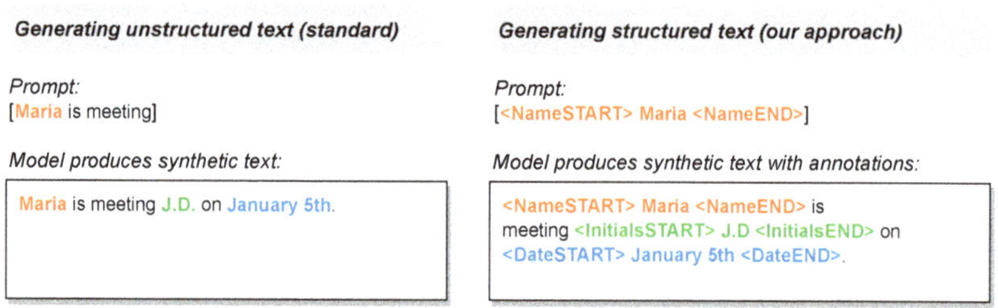

Figure 1. Illustrative example comparing standard text generation with the approach taken in this paper. We introduce special tokens to delimit protected health information (PHI). These tokens can be learned and generated like any other token by the language models. A prompt of three tokens defines the initial context.

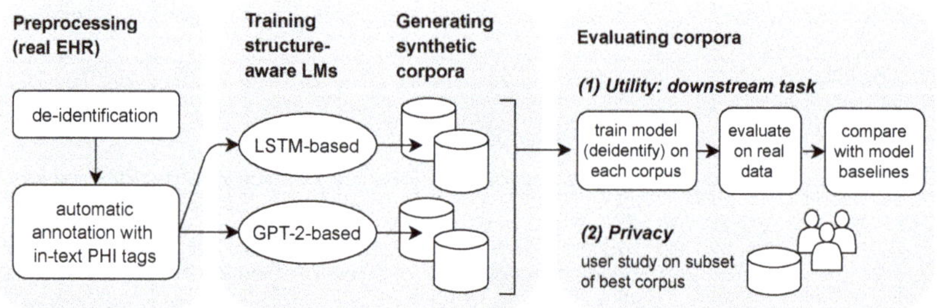

Figure 2. Overview of this study. (1) Raw, EHR text is automatically de-identified and annotated with in-text PHI labels. (2) Pre-processed text is used to train two "structure-aware" language models: an LSTM and GPT-2. (3) Using different decoding strategies, two synthetic corpora are generated from each language model. (4) Synthetic text is evaluated regarding utility and privacy. (4.1) Utility is measured by comparing the performance of machine learning models trained on synthetic data with models trained on real data. (4.2) For the privacy evaluation, ROUGE n-gram overlap and retrieval-based BM25 scoring is used to select the most similar real documents. Afterwards, the synthetic-real document pairs are presented to participants in a user study.

We compare two state-of-the-art language modeling approaches for the generation of synthetic EHR notes: a Long Short-Term Memory (LSTM) network [7] and a transformer-based network (GPT-2) [8]. To train these language models, we use a large and heterogeneous corpus of one million Dutch EHR notes. This dataset is unique in that it entails records of multiple institutions and care domains in the Netherlands.

We evaluate our approach by considering both utility and privacy of synthetic text. For utility, we choose the challenging NLP downstream task of de-identification. The objective of de-identification is to detect instances of protected health information (PHI) in text, such as names, dates, addresses and professions [9]. After detection, the PHI is masked or removed for privacy protection. De-identification as a downstream task is particularly interesting, because it requires sensitive data which would not be shared otherwise. We consider utility of synthetic data under two use-cases: (1) as a replacement for real data (e.g., in data sharing), and (2) as a data augmentation method to extend a (possibly small) set of real documents. To add in-text annotations for the de-identification downstream task, we obtain heuristic PHI annotations on the language model training data through a pre-trained de-identification method called "deidentify" [10]. Note that this setup is not limited to de-identification. In principle, any other information extraction method (or manual annotation) could act as a source for initial training annotations.

To evaluate privacy of synthetic records, we design a user study where participants are presented with the synthetic documents that entail the highest risks of privacy disclosure. As we have no 1-to-1 correspondence between real and synthetic documents, we devise a method to collect high-risk candidates for evaluation. We posit that synthetic documents with a high similarity to real documents have a higher risk of disclosing privacy sensitive information. We use ROUGE n-gram overlap [11] and retrieval-based BM25 scoring [12] to collect the set of candidate documents. Participants were asked to make judgments on the existence and replication of sensitive data in those examples with the goal to (1) evaluate the privacy of our synthetic data, and (2) to inform and motivate future research and privacy policies on the privacy risk assessment of free text that looks beyond PHI.

This paper makes the following contributions:

- We show that neural language models can be used successfully to generate artificial text with in-line annotations. Despite varying syntactic and stylistic properties, as well as topical incoherence, they are of sufficient utility to be used for training downstream machine learning models.
- Our user study provides insights into potential privacy threats associated with generative language models for synthetic EHR notes. These directly inform research on the development of automatic privacy evaluations for natural language.

We release the code of this study at: https://github.com/nedap/mdpi2021-textgen, accessed on 17 May 2021.

2. Background and Related Work

In this section, we provide a summary of related work on the generation of synthetic EHRs (Section 2.1), as well as the evaluation of privacy (Section 2.2). Furthermore, we give general background on language modeling and decoding methods (Section 2.3).

2.1. Generating Synthetic EHR Notes

The generation of synthetic EHR text for use in medical NLP is still at an early stage [3]. Most studies focus on the creation of English EHR text, using hospital discharge summaries from the MIMIC-III database [7,8,13,14]. In addition, a corpus of English Mental Health Records was explored [15]. Unlike the mixed healthcare data used in this study, these EHR notes have a more consistent, template-like structure and contain medical jargon, lending itself to clinical/biomedical downstream tasks found in related work [8,13–15]. Most of these studies focused on classification downstream tasks. To the best of our knowledge, we are the first study that attempts to generate synthetic data for sequence labeling (NER).

Decoding from language models is the predominant approach in related work to generate synthetic text. Approaches include unigram-language models and LSTMs [7], as well as transformer-based methods such as GPT-2 [13–15]. In particular, Amin-Nejad et al. [8] concluded that GPT-2 was suitable for text generation in a low-resource scenario. In this research, we compare a standard LSTM-based model with a transformer-based model (GPT-2). At the time this research was conducted, the only pre-trained Dutch transformer models available were BERT-based [16,17]. Since no pre-trained Dutch GPT-2 model existed, we chose to fine-tune an openly available English GPT-2 [6] on our data for this purpose.

Prior studies also consider different ways to generate EHR notes with a pre-defined topic. These approaches include conditional generation on clinical context [8,13] and guiding by keyphrases extracted from an original note [14,15,18]. As a result, the synthetic notes inherently have one-to-one relations with the original data. In this study, we do not use the conditional text generation approaches for two reasons. First, the NER use-case does not require strong guarantees on the topic of synthetic training examples. This is different from downstream tasks like classification. Second, we do not want that synthetic notes have a one-to-one link to real data. We assume that this benefits privacy protection. Instead of the conditional generation mentioned above, we use short prompts to generate whole EHR notes without a pre-defined topic.

2.2. Evaluating Privacy of Synthetic EHR Notes

While privacy preservation is one of the main motivations for the generation of synthetic EHR, related research did not always report privacy of generated corpora or propose methods for the evaluation. For example, Amin-Nejad et al. [8] and Liu [13] used similarity metrics as intrinsic measure to compare real and synthetic notes, but did not draw further conclusions on privacy. Melamud and Shivade [7] propose an empirical measure to quantify the risk of information leakage based on differential privacy. However, the calculation of this measure requires training a prohibitively large amount of models and does not directly provide information on the privacy of the generated data itself. Embedding differential privacy in the model training process, would theoretically ensure privacy [19]. However, the known trade-off between privacy and utility [7,19] dissuaded us from training differentially private models, as the primary focus was on achieving high utility. To draw conclusions about the privacy of our synthetic records, we develop a simple method to query "high-risk" candidates from the synthetic documents based on shallow text similarity metrics. We conduct a user study to investigate potential privacy issues concerning these records.

2.3. Background on Natural Language Generation

In the area of natural language generation (NLG) there are several approaches to generate artificial text. In this study, two neural methods with different architectures are considered, both of which are based on training a language model on text with the desired features (i.e., the one that we want to model). LSTM models are recurrent neural networks that process input sequentially and are able to learn long-term dependencies [20]. They are now widely used in natural language generation. More recently, Vaswani et al. [21] introduced the transformer architecture, which does not represent text sequentially, but can attend to the whole input in parallel and therefore store syntactic and semantic information on a higher level [6,21]. "GPT-2" or the "Generative Pre-Trained Transformer (2)" is an open-source, transformer-based language model by OpenAI [6], which was trained on 40 GB of text crawled from the internet. While already capable as a general-purpose model for English text [6], fine-tuning (i.e., transfer learning) can be used to learn a domain-specific language (e.g., non-English, medical jargon, writing style) while still taking advantage of the existing learned language patterns [22,23].

To use a language model for text generation, several decoding algorithms exist to pick a sequence of tokens that is likely to exist, given the language model. Depending on the chosen algorithm, the potential differences in outcome can be summarized as: (1) diversity, i.e., how much variation there is in different outputs, given the same input prompt, and (2) quality of the generated text, which may include how quickly it degrades with text length, and how meaningful, specific and repetitive it is [4,24–26]. As opposed to tasks like machine-translation (the output sequence must be consistent with the input sequence), open-ended language generation tasks demand higher diversity and creativity of output. Most commonly used are maximization-based decoding strategies (e.g., beam search).

However, these greedy methods tend to produce repetitive outputs. Sampling-based methods like temperature sampling and nucleus sampling generate more varied text [24].

3. Materials and Methods

This section describes our experimental setup including the dataset, procedure for training the language models and evaluation of utility and privacy.

3.1. Corpus for Language Modeling

To construct a large and heterogeneous dataset for language model training, we sample documents from the EHRs of 39 healthcare organizations in the Netherlands. Three domains of healthcare are represented within this sample: elderly care, mental care and disabled care. All text was written by trained care professionals such as nurses and general practitioners, and the language of reporting is Dutch. A wide variety of document types is present in this sample. This includes intake forms, progress notes, communications between care givers, and medical measurements. While some documents follow domain-specific conventions, the length, writing style and structure differs substantially across reports. The sample consists of 1.06 million reports with approximately 52 million tokens and a vocabulary size of 335 thousand. For language model training, we randomly split the dataset into training, validation, and testing sets with a 80/10/10 ratio. We received approval for the collection and use of the dataset from the privacy board of Nedap Healthcare.

3.2. Pre-Processing and Automatically Annotating the Language Modeling Data

Before using the collected real data for developing the language model, we pseudonymize it as follows. First, we detect PHI using a pre-trained de-identification tool for Dutch healthcare records called "deidentify" [10]. The "deidentify" model is a BiLSTM-CRF trained on Dutch healthcare records in the domains of elderly care, mental care and disabled care. The data is highly similar to the data used in this study and we expect comparable effectiveness to the results reported in the original paper (entity-level F1 of 0.893 [10]). After de-identfication, we replace the PHI with random, but realistic surrogates [27]. The surrogate PHI will serve as "ground-truth" annotations in the downstream NLP task (Section 3.4). Table 1 shows the distribution of PHI in the language modeling corpus. To make annotations explicitly part of the language modeling objective, we add in-text annotations from the PHI offsets (as shown in Figure 1). Each annotation is delimited by a special `<xSTART>` and `<xEND>` token where `x` stands for the entity type. We acknowledge that the automatically annotated PHI will be noisy. However, we assume that quality is sufficient for an initial exploration of the viability of our synthetic data generation approach. Unless otherwise stated, we use the spaCy (https://github.com/explosion/spaCy, accessed on 19 May 2021) tokenizer and replace newlines with a `<PAR>` token.

We would like to highlight the motivation for annotating the real documents (i.e., before language modeling) and not the synthetic documents (i.e., after language generation). In theory, because we have a pre-trained NER model available, both options are possible. However, there are two reasons why we propose to make the annotations part of the language modeling. First, the language models may learn to generate novel entities that a pre-trained model would not detect (we provide tentative evidence for this in Section 4.2.2). Second, because we could generate synthetic datasets many orders of magnitude larger than the source data, it is more efficient to annotate the language modeling data. The second argument especially holds if no pre-trained annotation model is available and records have to be manually annotated.

Table 1. Distribution of PHI tags in the 52 million token corpus used to develop the language models (i.e., real data). PHI was tagged by an automatic de-identification routine.

PHI Tag	Count	% of Total
Name	782,499	59.74
Date	202,929	15.49
Initials	181,811	13.88
Address	46,387	3.54
Care Institute	38,669	2.95
Organization	37,284	2.85
Internal Location	6977	0.53
Phone/Fax	3843	0.29
Age	3350	0.26
Email	2539	0.19
Hospital	2425	0.19
Profession	537	0.04
URL/IP	326	0.02
ID	232	0.02
Other	105	0.01
SSN	6	0.00
Total	1,309,919	100

3.3. *Generative Language Models*

We compare two language modeling approaches for the generation of synthetic corpora: LSTM-based [20] and transformer-based (GPT-2) [6]. Below, we outline the model architectures as well as the decoding methods to generate four synthetic corpora. For a summary, see Tables 2 and 3.

3.3.1. LSTM-Based Model

Because of their success in generating English EHR, we re-implement the method including hyperparameters by Melamud and Shivade [7]. The model is a 2-layer LSTM with 650 hidden-units, an embedding layer of size 650 and a softmax output layer. Input and output weights are tied. The model is trained for 50 epochs using vanilla gradient descent, a batch size of 20 and a sequence length of 35. We also use learning rate back-off from [7]. The initial learning rate is set to 20 and reduced by a factor of 4 after every epoch where the validation loss did not decrease. The minimum learning rate is set to 0.1. For efficiency reasons, we replace tokens that occur fewer than 10 times in the training data with `<unk>` [7].

3.3.2. Transformer-Based Model (GPT-2)

From the family of transformer models, we use GPT-2 [6]. Prior work showed promising results using GPT-2 for the generation of English EHR [8]. To the best of our knowledge, there is no Dutch GPT-2 model for the clinical domain which we could re-use. However, prior work showed that pre-trained English models can be adapted to the Dutch language with smaller computational demand than training from scratch [28]. The intuition is, that the Dutch and English language share similar language rules and even (sub-)words. Below, we provide a summary of this fine-tuning process.

Adapting the vocabulary: We train a byte-pair-encoding (BPE) tokenizer on our Dutch EHR corpus. All sub-word embeddings are randomly initialized. To benefit from the pre-trained English GPT-2 model (small variant) [6], we copy embeddings that are shared between the English and Dutch tokenizer. To account for the in-text annotations, we add a tokenization rule to not split PHI tags into sub-words.

Fine-tuning the model: The layers of the pre-trained GPT-2 model represent text at different abstraction levels. For transfer learning, the key is to take advantage of the previously learned information that is relevant for the current task, but adjust representations such that they are suitable for the new language and domain-specific terminology. To do so, layers are split into groups and we use gradual unfreezing with differential learning rates, such that the last layer group (with corpus-specific information) is changed more than the first ones, where learned representations can be re-used. To train layer groups on our data, we used the one-cycle-policy [29], where learning rates are scheduled with cosine annealing. Our GPT-2 model was split into four layer groups which were trained in 5 epochs. We provide additional details on model and fine-tuning steps in Table 2 and Appendix A.

Table 2. Summary of language models used to generate synthetic text. Note that the test perplexity cannot be directly compared due to the difference in vocabulary.

	LSTM	**GPT2**
Tokenizer	spaCy, replace low-frequency tokens (<= 10) with `<unk>`	Trained English "ByteLevelBPE Tokenizer" on Dutch corpus, while keeping embeddings for common tokens.
Model	2-layer LSTM (650 input embedding size, 650 hidden units, softmax output) [7]	GPT-2 English small (12-layer, 768-hidden, 12-heads, 117M parameters before fine-tuning) [6]
Vocabulary	49,978 tokens	50,257 tokens
Parameters	39,307,380	163,037,184 (after fine-tuning)
Perplexity	32.1	38.8

3.3.3. Decoding Methods for Generation of Synthetic Corpora

Using the LSTM, GPT-2 and different decoding methods, we generated four synthetic corpora of approximately 1 million tokens each (Table 3). As initial context for each report, we selected random prompts of length 3. These were sampled from held-out EHRs to minimize the possibility of reconstructing real documents during generation. Generation of a text was terminated either when a maximum token count was reached, or when the model produced an end-of-document token. For all corpora, we impose a subjective minimum document length of 50 tokens.

Following Holtzman et al. [24], we generate two corpora with nucleus sampling ($p = 0.95$, LSTM-p and GPT-p). Additionally, we implement the decoding methods of the papers that proposed the LSTM [7] and GPT-2 [8] for the generation of EHRs. For the LSTM, we generate a corpus with temperature sampling ($t = 1$, LSTM-temp). For the GPT-2 we use beam search ($n = 5$, GPT-beam) and exclude texts without PHI tags, as the corpus already had a lower overall number of tags which are essential for the utility in the downstream task. For both GPT-2 corpora, we set the generator to not repeat n-grams longer than 2 words within one text to increase variability. In rare cases, the language models produced annotations with trailing start/end tags. These malformed annotations were removed in an automatic post-processing step. We quantify how many annotations were removed in Section 4.1.1.

Table 3. Overview of language model decoding parameters to generate four synthetic corpora.

Corpus	**Model**	**Generation Method**	**Tokens/Doc.**
LSTM-p	LSTM	p-sampling ($p = 0.95$)	50–400
LSTM-temp	LSTM	Temperature sampling ($t = 1$)	50–500
GPT-p	GPT-2	p-sampling ($p = 0.95$)	50–400
GPT-beam	GPT-2	Beam search (beams $n = 5$)	50–500

3.4. *Extrinsic Evaluation on NLP Downstream Task*

To understand if the synthetic data and annotations have sufficient utility to be used for training of NLP models, we measure effectiveness in a de-identification downstream task. The objective of de-identification is to detect instances of PHI in text, such as names, dates, addresses and professions [9]. Ideally, a de-identification model trained on synthetic data performs as good or better than a model trained on real data. To evaluate this, we train a BiLSTM-CRF de-identification model in three settings: (1) using real data, (2) extending real with synthetic data, and (3) using only synthetic data (Figure 3). As implementation for the BiLSTM-CRF, we use "deidentify" (https://github.com/nedap/deidentify, accessed on 19 May 2021) with the same architecture and hyperparameters as reported in the original paper [10]. As real data, we use the NUT corpus of that study with the same test split such that results are comparable. NUT consists of 1260 records with gold-standard PHI annotations.

The effectiveness of the de-identification models is measured by entity-level precision, recall and F1. The BiLSTM-CRF trained on real data is considered as the upper baseline for this problem. We also report scores of a rule-based system (DEDUCE [30]) which gives a performance estimate in the absence of any real or synthetic training data.

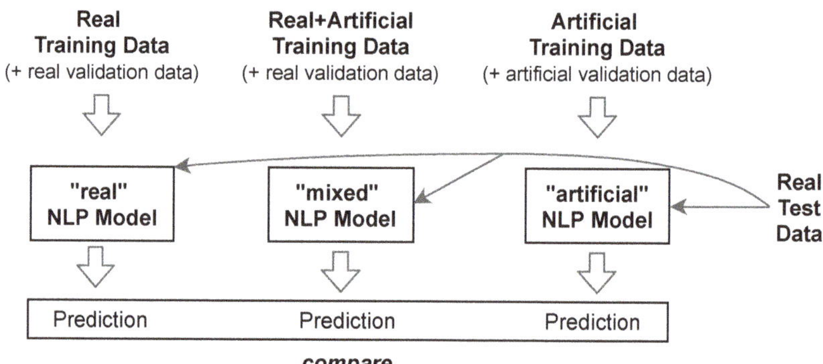

Figure 3. Overview of extrinsic evaluation procedure. We compare three settings: (1) a model trained on real data (baseline), (2) a "mixed" case, where we extend real data with synthetic data, and (3) only synthetic training data. All models were tested on real data (gold annotations). This evaluation setup extends Ive et al. [15] by step (2).

3.5. Privacy Evaluation

To gain insights into the privacy of synthetic data, we conducted a user study for a subset of synthetic documents from the corpus with highest utility in the downstream task. Our goal was to check whether any information "leaked" from the real data into the synthetic data, and whether this information could be used to re-identify an individual.

Finding potential worst cases for privacy. The assumption is that a privacy leak may have occurred when certain information of a real document reappears in a synthetic document. Similarly to the study by Choi et al. [31], we have no 1-to-1 correspondence between real and synthetic records. Let $s \in S$ be a synthetic document and $r \in R$ be a real document. Assuming that the likelihood of a privacy leak is higher when the proximity between s and r is high, we get a set of document pairs (SR) where for each s the most similar document r is retrieved as candidate source document (cf. Figure 4). We use three measures to obtain the most similar documents to a synthetic document: ROUGE-N recall [11], with $n = 3$ and with $n = 5$, and retrieval-based BM25 scoring [12]. We use standard BM25 parameters $b = 0.75$ and $k = 1.2$ [12].

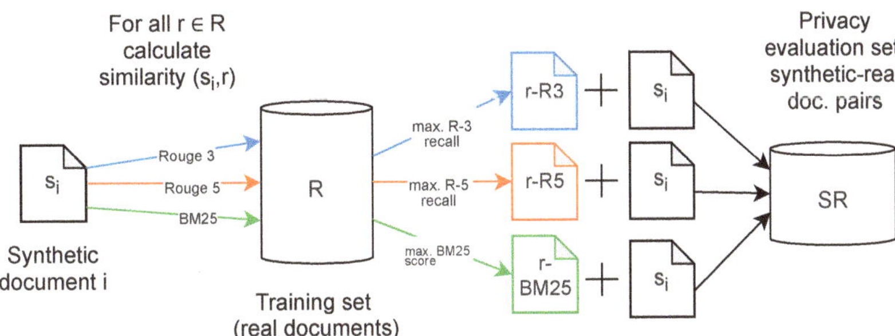

Figure 4. Illustration of method used to compile a set of similar synthetic-real document pairs for the privacy evaluation. For each synthetic document, we retrieve the most similar source documents from the real data, based on ROUGE n-gram overlap and BM25. The set SR contains the pooled result of this matching process, such that each synthetic document appears in three separate pairings: once with the top ROUGE-3 match, once with the top ROUGE-5 match and once with the top BM25 match.

Instead of randomly sampling synthetic documents for manual inspection, we used several filtering steps to maximize the probability of showing pairs with high similarity and readability during evaluation: We first sorted the documents by highest ROUGE scores. Afterwards, we removed duplicates, documents longer than 1000 characters (to control the reading effort of participants), and documents that received high similarity scores mostly based on structural elements (e.g., `<PAR>` tokens). We took the top 122 documents with highest ROUGE score for the user study. Full details of the filtering procedure are provided in Appendix D.

Participants were asked to answer the following questions for each pair of real/synthetic documents:

Q1: "Do you think the real doc provides enough information to identify a person?"
Q2: "Do you think the synthetic doc contains person identifying information?"
Q3: "Do you think that there is a link between the synthetic and real doc in the sense that it may identify someone in the real doc?"
Q4: "Please motivate your answer for Q3."

Questions 1–3 are on a 5-point Likert scale (Yes, Probably yes, Not sure, Probably not, No), and Q4 is an open text answer. Participants received a short introduction about the task and privacy. We supplied two trial documents for participants to get used to the task. These documents were excluded from analysis. The full questionnaire and participation instructions are given in Appendix D.

As the privacy sensitive data could not be shared with external parties, we recruited 12 participants from our institution (Nedap Healthcare). Due to the participant pool, there is a potential bias for technical and care related experts. We consider the impact for a privacy evaluation low, and indeed, because of their domain knowledge, participants have provided some helpful domain-related qualitative feedback. All participants were native Dutch speakers and each document pair was independently examined by two participants. We computed inter-participant agreement for each question with Cohen's Kappa. As the Likert scales produce ordinal data and there is a natural and relevant rank-order, we also calculated the Spearman's Rank-Order Correlation, to better capture the difference in participants disagreeing by, for example, answering "Yes" and "Probably" versus "Yes" and "No." This is especially relevant for the questions in this evaluation, which are hard to answer and likely to result in participants showing different levels of confidence due to personal differences. Both Kappa score and Spearman correlation were calculated per question, micro-averaged over all document pairs.

4. Results

In this section, we provide a quantitative and qualitative analysis of the generated synthetic data (Section 4.1). Afterwards, we discuss the utility of these data in the de-identification downstream task (Section 4.2). We conclude with the results of our user study on the privacy of synthetic documents (Section 4.3).

4.1. Does the Synthetic Data Resemble the Properties of Real Data?

For an ideal data generation method, we would expect that the synthesized data closely follows the characteristics of real data. We examine key summary statistics for each synthetic corpus and give a real corpus as reference (Table 4).

We make two observations. First, the synthetic corpora differ substantially in variety as quantified by the vocabulary size. At the extremes, the vocabulary of LSTM-temp is 3.7 times larger than the vocabulary of GPT-beam although they are comparable in size (approximately 1 million tokens). We expect that the variety has implications for the downstream utility of the datasets. Second, the GPT-2 p-sampling method generates sentences that are on average shorter than those of other methods. It is unclear what causes this specific behavior, but it indicates that the methods learn a different syntactic and stylistic representation of text. In summary, the synthetic text deviates from real text in key metrics. We investigate if it is still useful for downstream tasks in Section 4.2.

Table 4. Summary statistics of the synthetic corpora in reference to a real corpus (NUT).

	NUT [10]	**LSTM-p**	**LSTM-Temp**	**GPT-p**	**GPT-Beam**
Tokens	445,586	976,637	977,583	1,087,887	1,045,359
Vocabulary	30,252	23,052	29,485	12,149	8026
PHI instances	17,464	32,639	31,776	105,121	24,470
Sentences	43,682	70,527	72,140	128,773	83,634
Avg. tokens per sentence	10.2	13.8	13.6	8.4	12.5

4.1.1. Are the Synthetic PHI Annotations Well-Formed and Realistically Represented?

The syntactic quality of PHI annotations is good across all corpora. Between 97% and 99% of the annotations were well-formed (Table 5). We observe that the LSTM-based generators are slightly more consistent than the GPT-based generators. With respect to the distribution of PHI types, we observe that LSTM-based corpora stay closer to the real distribution (Figure 5). The GPT-2 model with beam-search decoder shows a pronounced bias for "Date" while the GPT-2 model with p-sampling boosts some of the rare PHI tags. Additionally, we note that the GPT-p corpus has substantially more PHI annotations (105 k) than the other corpora (24 k–33 k, Table 4). We analyze the impact of this in context of the downstream task (Section 4.2). A detailed report on the PHI frequencies per corpus can be found in Appendix B.

Table 5. A comparison of PHI tag consistency across synthetic corpora.

	LSTM-p	**LSTM-Temp**	**GPT-p**	**GPT-Beam**
Well-formed PHI tags	99.97%	99.89%	97.75%	98.84%
Malformed PHI tags	0.03%	0.11%	2.25%	1.16%

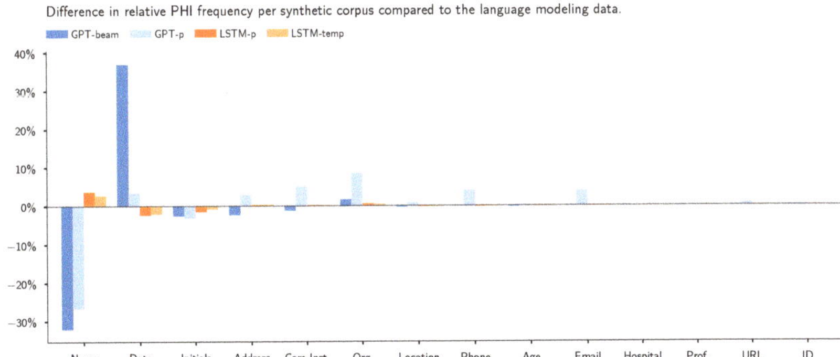

Figure 5. How well do the synthetic corpora reflect the real PHI distribution? This figure shows the differences to the PHI distribution of the language model training data (cf. Table 1).

4.1.2. Is the Generated Text Semantically Coherent?

To get a better understanding of the quality of generated text, we manually inspected random documents of the synthetic corpora (examples in Figure 6 and Appendix C). We make the following observations: while most texts are syntactically correct, the majority is incoherent. We hypothesize that the incoherence is caused by the large variety of reporting styles in the training corpus. This may have inhibited the language models to learn a specific type of text more accurately. Furthermore, we observe some replication of templates and phrases of real documents. An example of this is shown in Figure 6. This was most evident for texts generated by the GPT-2 with beam search. We give additional examples in Appendix C where we used the same prompt to generate text with all four approaches. In those examples, the LSTM texts are more varied, but also less coherent compared to the GPT-2 texts. Most notably, as the text length increases, the LSTM tends to deviate from the original context of the prompt while the GPT-2 stays closer to the topic.

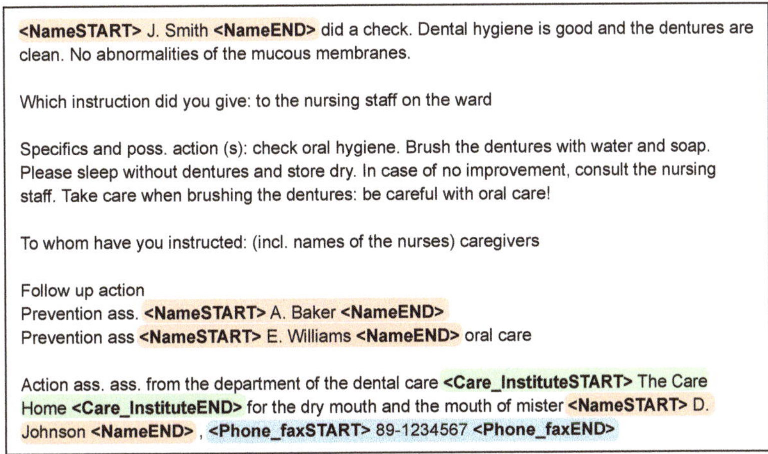

<NameSTART> J. Smith **<NameEND>** did a check. Dental hygiene is good and the dentures are clean. No abnormalities of the mucous membranes.

Which instruction did you give: to the nursing staff on the ward

Specifics and poss. action (s): check oral hygiene. Brush the dentures with water and soap. Please sleep without dentures and store dry. In case of no improvement, consult the nursing staff. Take care when brushing the dentures: be careful with oral care!

To whom have you instructed: (incl. names of the nurses) caregivers

Follow up action
Prevention ass. **<NameSTART>** A. Baker **<NameEND>**
Prevention ass **<NameSTART>** E. Williams **<NameEND>** oral care

Action ass. ass. from the department of the dental care **<Care_InstituteSTART>** The Care Home **<Care_InstituteEND>** for the dry mouth and the mouth of mister **<NameSTART>** D. Johnson **<NameEND>** , **<Phone_faxSTART>** 89-1234567 **<Phone_faxEND>**

Figure 6. Text sample from the GPT-beam corpus (translated from Dutch, PHI highlighted and replaced with random identifiers). The structure of the generated text resembles a template that nurses used in the real data to report on dental hygiene of a patient.

4.2. Extrinsic Evaluation: Is the Utility of Synthetic Data Sufficient for Downstream Use?

We discuss the utility of synthetic data by considering two use cases: (1) as a replacement for real data, when real data are unavailable or cannot be shared, and (2) as a special form of data augmentation to generate cheap additional training examples.

4.2.1. Using Synthetic Data as a Replacement for Real Data

We find that de-identification models trained on any of the four synthetic corpora are not as effective as the real-data baseline (Table 6). However, the results are promising. In particular, the synthetic models outperform the rule-based method DEDUCE [30] by a large margin because of a substantial increase in recall (56.4% vs. 77.3% for LSTM-temp). The rule-based method relies on domain knowledge rather than real training examples and is therefore an interesting reference when no real training data is available. Overall, we observe that the LSTM-corpora provide better utility compared to the GPT-2 corpora, both in precision and recall (Table 6). Note that this is despite our earlier finding that the LSTM-corpora are less coherent (Section 4.1.2). For a task like de-identification, it seems that syntactic correctness is more important than coherency.

We study the influence of different PHI distributions in synthetic data by measuring precision and recall on a PHI-level (Table 7). We find that the de-identification model trained on LSTM data performs well on tags that appear frequently in the real data (e.g., Name and Date). However, the coverage of infrequent tags is insufficient (e.g., phone/fax and email). In contrast, the model trained on GPT-2 data is slightly less effective on the majority of PHI tags, but has a greater coverage of tags. We attribute this behavior to the GPT-2 p-sampling decoder, which seemingly boosted some of the rare PHI tags as discussed in Section 4.1.1. Considering the low effectiveness for identity-revealing tags, training de-identification models only on synthetic data is not yet practical. This is due to the high recall requirement for this task.

Table 6. Summary of downstream task performance. We train on the generated synthetic data and evaluate on real data with gold-standard annotations (*NUT* dataset [10]). Statistically significant improvements toward the *NUT (BiLSTM-CRF)* baseline are marked with ▲, and ° depicts no significant difference. The test is a two-tailed approximate randomization ($p < 0.01$).

Split: Train/val/Test	Dataset	Precision	Recall	F1
-/-/real	NUT (rule-based) [30]	0.807	0.564	0.664
real/real/real	NUT (BiLSTM-CRF) [10]	**0.925**	0.867	0.895
Use case 1: synthetic data as a replacement for real data				
synth/synth/real	LSTM-p	0.835	0.784	0.809
synth/synth/real	LSTM-temp	0.857	0.773	0.813
synth/synth/real	GPT-p	0.776	0.700	0.736
synth/synth/real	GPT-beam	0.823	0.688	0.749
Use case 2: synthetic data as data augmentation method				
real+synth/real/real	NUT+LSTM-temp	0.919°	**0.883**▲	**0.901**°
real+synth/real/real	NUT+LSTM-p	0.916°	0.879▲	0.897°

Finally, recall from Section 3.3.3 that we set the size of the synthetic corpora to 1 million tokens for all corpora. To understand how this setting influences the effectiveness of the downstream model, we train de-identification models on subsets of the synthetic data (LSTM-p corpus). We find that the learning curve flattens when using around 70% of the training data. This indicates that generating more data will not necessarily increase effectiveness. See Appendix E for details on this experiment.

Table 7. Entity-level precision and recall per PHI category. Comparing the baseline (*NUT*) with two models trained and validated on pure synthetic data (LSTM-p vs. GPT-p), as well as the mixed variant (NUT+LSTM-p) where the training set is composed of NUT and LSTM-p, but the validation set is the same as the one used in the baseline (real data). Highlighted values (bold) show improvements over the *NUT* baseline.

PHI Tag	NUT		GPT-p		LSTM-p		NUT+LSTM-p	
	Prec.	Rec.	Prec.	Rec.	Prec.	Rec.	Prec.	Rec.
Name	0.967	0.951	0.810	0.875	0.897	0.945	0.960	**0.959**
Date	0.929	0.910	0.910	0.813	0.889	**0.913**	**0.932**	**0.920**
Initials	0.896	0.629	0.456	0.146	0.595	0.421	0.822	**0.674**
Address	0.888	0.814	0.460	0.654	0.716	0.680	**0.901**	**0.878**
Care Institute	0.742	0.681	0.321	0.116	0.414	0.245	0.705	**0.718**
Organization	0.743	0.596	0.159	0.052	0.340	0.257	0.717	0.559
Internal Location	0.784	0.527	0.273	0.055	0.188	0.055	0.757	0.509
Phone/Fax	1.000	1.000	1.000	0.563	0.000	0.000	0.941	1.000
Age	0.757	0.683	0.320	0.195	**0.786**	0.268	**0.758**	0.610
Email	0.909	1.000	**1.000**	1.000	0.000	0.000	0.833	1.000
Hospital	0.778	0.700	0.333	0.100	0.300	0.300	**0.857**	0.600
Profession	0.833	0.238	0.000	0.000	0.000	0.000	**0.923**	**0.286**
URL/IP	1.000	0.750	1.000	0.500	0.000	0.000	1.000	0.750
ID	0.714	0.400	0.500	0.080	0.000	0.000	**0.786**	**0.440**
Other	0.000	0.000	0.000	0.000	0.000	0.000	0.000	0.000

4.2.2. Using Synthetic Data as Data Augmentation Method

As data annotation for de-identification is an expensive process, we experiment with a dataset that combines a small set of real documents (NUT) with a large set of synthetic documents. In this case, we focus on the synthetic corpora that showed best extrinsic utility (LSTM-temp and LSTM-p). We find that the combined datasets result in models with statistically significant improvements in recall with only an insignificant decrease in precision (Table 6). This increase in recall indicates that the language model produced novel PHI that was absent from the real training documents (NUT). At an entity level, we also observe that almost all PHI classes benefit from additional training examples (Table 7). Note that this performance improvement was achieved without additional manual annotation effort. The absence of an even larger improvement may be caused by a saturation of the model with only real data. Indeed, Trienes et al. [10] reported F1-scores for varying training set sizes (given real data), which show that at 100% of the training set, the learning curve has flattened.

4.3. *Privacy Findings: Was Sensitive Information Leaked into the Synthetic Records?*

The goal of the privacy evaluation was to learn whether the synthetic corpus (in this case the one with the highest utility, LSTM-p) contains documents that could leak privacy sensitive information from the real data. We sampled the synthetic-real document pairs with highest similarity and conducted a user study to find out what is considered person identifying information and whether there are cases where privacy has been compromised in the synthetic corpus.

4.3.1. Similarity between Real and Synthetic Documents

To give a first indication of potential privacy leaks, we report summary statistics for the ROUGE-N recall between all pairs of real/synthetic documents (Table 8). On average, the low n-gram recall suggests that the synthetic data is substantially different from the real data. However, we also find "high-risk cases" with large n-gram overlap. In some rare cases, documents were reproduced exactly (maximum ROUGE-N recall of 1). We focus on the top 122 synthetic documents with highest risk in the user study.

Table 8. Summary statistics for ROUGE-N recall over all real/synthetic document pairs and over the filtered subset of "high-risk" documents presented to participants in the user study.

	Over All Real/Synthetic Pairs				Over 122 "High-Risk" Pairs			
	Avg.	Median	Min.	Max.	Avg.	Median	Min.	Max.
ROUGE-3 recall	0.075	0.067	0.018	1.000	0.280	0.217	0.145	1.000
ROUGE-5 recall	0.031	0.026	0.000	1.000	0.207	0.143	0.025	1.000

4.3.2. User Study

Question 1 (Information to Re-Identify a Person in Real Document)

There was a fair agreement between participants (Cohen's Kappa $\kappa = 0.279$). The Spearman's rank-order coefficient of $\rho = 0.488$ (with $p = 1.19 \times 10^{-8}$) suggests that there is a (monotonic) positive association between the ratings of both participants. In 53 of 122 cases (Figure 7), participants agreed that the real document did not provide enough information to identify a person. In cases where participants answered with either "Probably" or "Yes," text often contained specific diagnoses (e.g., decubitus) in conjunction with PHI. Other examples were documents with specific psychological examination results (e.g., on personality, existence of suicidal thoughts, cognition, affect) or detailed descriptions of rare events (e.g., a person leaving a care home, an individual running away, descriptions of aggressive behavior). This highlights the concern that the removal of PHI in free text may not be sufficient to make it anonymous. A reader who might have been present during a described event could potentially re-identify a person without direct identifiers, if the event was unique enough.

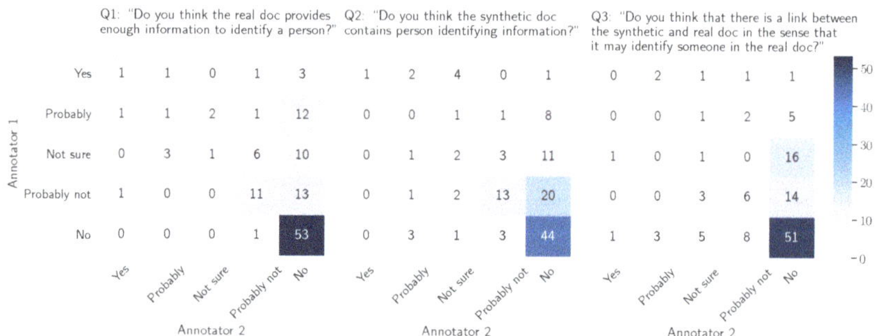

Figure 7. Inter-participant agreement (count of answer given) for the user study on privacy.

Question 2 (Information to Re-Identify a Person in Synthetic Document)

Similarly to the inter-participator agreement for question 1, Cohen's Kappa showed a fair agreement ($\kappa = 0.215$). Spearman's rank-order coefficient was $\rho = 0.4757$ ($p = 3.07 \times 10^{-8}$). The confusion matrix of participant responses in Figure 7 reveals that also for the synthetic documents shown, the contained information was often not considered person identifying. Some comments given for question 3 indicate that part of the reason may be the general incoherence of details that shows that the text is clearly fake and not about one specific person, thereby obfuscating which information is real and which PHI is related to it. For example, a text may reference several different names that do not fit together in context. This creates a privacy-protecting effect where information cannot be linked to one specific person. Furthermore, synthetic reports were often generic descriptions of days and medications without any identifiers. In cases where participants disagreed, but at least one answered with "Probably" or "Yes," reports were generally detailed and could contain person identifiers.

Question 3 (Identifying a Link between Real and Synthetic Document)

There was a slight agreement between participants ($\kappa = 0.063$ and $\rho = 0.4104$ with $p = 3 \times 10^{-6}$). In 42% of cases (51 of 122, Figure 7) both participants agreed that there was no link between the real and synthetic document. In cases where both participants agreed on the direction, but not strength of judgment and answered "Yes" or "Probably," the additional explanations revealed three categories of how synthetic text may identify someone from the real document:

1. **Contextual information was copied.** For example, the synthetic and real document described similar treatment, schedule or complications, sometimes with largely identical text including medical test results. One participant pointed out that the severity of this case would depend on the uniqueness of the medical test.
2. **Identifiers were copied.** For example, the same name(s) appeared in both documents. Unless contextual information was replicated, participants often disagreed on the severity of a potential privacy leak.
3. **The synthetic document acted as continuation of the real document with linked information**. Counterarguments to the existence of a privacy breach included inconsistencies in synthetic text that made it appear clearly fake (see Question 2) and generic content that made it hard to say whether a description was about the same person or not.

There were two examples in which participants agreed on a privacy breach. These contained specific descriptions of a diagnosis or situation that seemed unique enough to lead back to a person (e.g., someone dying soon, if in a non-dying population) and were copied from the original to a large extent. Interestingly, while the incoherence of certain synthetic text often added as protective factor for privacy, the effect may be reversed when a part of text is clearly fake and another part is clearly real, making it possible for a potential attacker to easily pick out copied information.

The findings of the privacy evaluation can be summarized as follows:

- In free text, the removal of PHI may not be sufficient to protect privacy when specific and rare events are described in detail.
- The mediocre quality of synthetic text often acted as protective factor by obfuscating what is real and what is fake.
- The largest cause of concern for privacy in this synthetic corpus is the existence of larger chunks of text that were copied from the real data, especially when rare events were described.

5. Implications and Outlook

In this section, we discuss the broader implications of our results and suggest avenues for future work to improve both utility and privacy of synthetic data.

5.1. Synthetic Data Generation and Text Quality

Controlling the distribution of annotations: We showed that it is possible to generate well-structured in-text annotations. However, we also observed that the distribution of tags depends on the chosen decoding method. This, in turn, had substantial impact on performance in downstream tasks. A desirable feature for generation methods is therefore the ability to control this distribution. Preliminary work in this direction, namely conditional transformer models [32,33], could be adapted for this purpose.

Increasing text diversity: Our experiments also revealed that text diversity has a significant impact on downstream task performance. In particular, we found that sampling methods provided both higher diversity and utility compared to beam search, which is in line with other results on open-ended text generation [24]. We think that future studies should strive to further increase the diversity of text. One promising direction is the so-called "unlikelihood training" proposed by Welleck et al. [26], which increases diversity by changing the language modeling objective.

Improving text quality: The primary focus of this study was to generate documents with high utility for NLP models. Consequently, medical correctness and coherency was not formally evaluated. However, we found the coherence of synthetic documents to be mediocre. Related studies on generation of English EHR (mostly based on discharge letters in MIMIC-III) did not report such issues [7,8,13,14]. A key difference between MIMIC-III discharge letters and our Dutch healthcare corpus is the lack of clear structure and conformity in the Dutch corpus. To make methods for synthetic EHR generation applicable across healthcare, it would be beneficial to explore different pre-processing or model training strategies. One viable option could be to train separate models on subsets of notes that share structural properties.

Quantify how heuristic annotations influence downstream NER methods: We used a pre-trained method to automatically add in-text annotations to the language modeling data. While the pre-trained method showed high effectiveness ($F_1 = 0.895$, cf. Table 6) on highly similar data, we acknowledge that the annotations are imperfect. Therefore, it would be interesting to quantify how the accuracy of the in-text annotations influences the effectiveness of downstream NER models. As we are constrained by annotation resources, we leave the exploration of this idea to future research.

Transfer of method to other languages and domains: Instead of generating synthetic healthcare data for the Dutch language, the methodology of this research can also be used for different languages and text types: We trained the LSTM from scratch and since the architecture is not language specific, it may be applied to any sequence of tokens. Tokenization is language dependent, so pre-processing should be adjusted accordingly. We also fine-tuned the English pre-trained GPT-2 model and its tokenizer to learn Dutch, domain specific language and special annotations. This was possible, because there are similarities between Dutch and English. Sufficient similarity also exists with other languages, some of which GPT-2 has been adapted to previously (e.g., Italian [23,28]) and some open-source GPT-2 models pre-trained in different languages are openly available (e.g., a German pre-trained GPT-2 model: https://github.com/stefan-it/german-gpt2, accessed on 19 May 2021). GPT-2 is a "general purpose" model [6], because it can be adapted to different domains and language generation tasks, so cross-domain training is generally possible. While transfer of both LSTM and GPT-2 to other languages and domains is possible, applications that require generation of longer texts may require adjustments to the methodology (e.g., story generation [18]).

Support of other NLP downstream tasks: We investigated synthetic data generation in the context of de-identification. As de-identification is phrased as a standard NER task, we expect that our method generalizes well to other NER tasks. Future work is needed to investigate if language models can be adapted to produce other types of document metadata to support additional NLP downstream tasks such as classification.

5.2. Privacy of Synthetic Text

Privacy/utility trade-off: Our experiments showed that synthetic text does not need to be realistic for utility in downstream NER tasks. This could be exploited to improve the privacy protection. For example, a clearly incoherent combination of names within a document would obfuscate how pieces of information were originally linked. Therefore, future work could investigate how realistic synthetic text needs to be for a given downstream task. Prior work studied the trade-off between perplexity and privacy [7], where perplexity is a proxy for utility. This approach could be extended to take utility of synthetic text into account.

Expanding de-identification: Current approaches to text anonymization mostly define PHI as the 18-categories set out by the HIPAA regulation [34]. For example, documents in MIMIC-III are shared under the promise that all PHI have been removed and therefore protect privacy sufficiently. However, disregarding whether text was real or synthetic, our user study identified certain aspects of notes which are not covered by automatic PHI extraction methods. Therefore, the common approach to protect privacy in natural language text might have to be re-evaluated and expanded to take, for example, specific descriptions of unusual events into account.

Embedding privacy: Given the examples of privacy leaks identified in the user study, it seemed that most would have been prevented if the model could not reproduce larger text chunks from a training EHR note. A way to ensure this from a mathematical perspective is to train the generative models with a differential privacy (DP) objective. The premise of DP is that no output could be directly attributed to a single training instance [2,7,19,35]. In this study, we consciously chose not to include DP to maximize the utility of the synthetic corpora for the downstream task, but we recommend that future research uses DP in order to minimize privacy risks.

Limitations of user study: While our user study provides insights into the privacy of synthetic records, it does not allow us to draw conclusions on the privacy of a synthetic corpus at large. To be able to publish synthetic corpora under the premise that they protect privacy of data subjects, principled ways of measuring the involved privacy risks are needed. Developing these approaches is an important direction for future work.

6. Conclusions

This paper proposes the use of language models to generate synthetic EHRs. By explicitly adding in-text annotations to the training data, the language models learn to produce artificial text that is automatically annotated for downstream NER tasks. Our experiments show that the synthetic data are of sufficient utility for downstream use in de-identification. In particular, a de-identification method trained on synthetic data outperforms a rule-based method. Moreover, augmenting real data with synthetic data further improves the recall of the method at no additional costs or manual annotation effort. We find that the LSTM-based method produces synthetic text with higher utility in the downstream task compared to GPT-2. This is despite the fact that GPT-2 texts are more coherent. This suggests that coherence is not required for synthetic text to be useful in downstream NER tasks. We furthermore evaluate privacy of the generated synthetic data using text-proximity metrics and conduct a user study. We find that the synthetic documents are not free of privacy concerns because language models replicated potentially identifying chunks of real EHRs. This shows that additional work is needed before synthetic EHRs can be used as an anonymous alternative to real text in data sharing settings.

Author Contributions: Conceptualization, C.A.L., J.T., D.T., C.S.; methodology C.A.L., J.T., D.T., C.S.; software, C.A.L.; writing—original draft, C.A.L., J.T.; writing—review and editing, J.T., D.T., C.S.; supervision, C.S. All authors have read and agreed to the published version of the manuscript.

Funding: We acknowledge support by the Open Access Publication Fund of the University of Duisburg-Essen.

Data Availability Statement: The data used in this study was pseudonymized for privacy protection. We received approval for the collection and use of the dataset from the privacy board of Nedap Healthcare. Because of privacy regulations, the dataset cannot be made publicly available.

Conflicts of Interest: The authors declare no conflict of interest.

Appendix A. Fine-Tuning English GPT-2 to Dutch Language

This appendix provides additional information on how we adapted the English GPT-2 model to Dutch healthcare data. At the time when we conducted this research, no study reported the code or a detailed strategy to adapt GPT-2 for a non-English purpose. Therefore, we followed the approach described by Pierre Guilliou adapting GPT-2 to Portuguese. The report can be found here: https://medium.com/@pierre_guillou/faster-than-training-from-scratch-fine-tuning-the-english-gpt-2-in-any-language-with-hugging-f2ec05c98787, accessed on 19 May 2021. The approach is similar to the work (published later) by de Vries and Nissim [28]. Below, we outline how the tokenizer was extended to the Dutch vocabulary and provide the fine-tuning steps in Table A1.

1. Settings of the Byte-Pair Encoding (BPE) tokenizer: Initial size equals to vocabulary length $|V|$ of English pre-trained GPT-2 tokenizer. Minimum token frequency is set to 2. We add a prefix space as well as special tokens for PHI tags and paragraph delimiters (e.g., `<PAR>`, `<NameSTART>`, `<NameEND>`). Sequences are truncated with a maximum sequence length of 1024. Padding token is set to `<|endoftext|>`.
2. New word-token-embedding matrix is initialized by copying English embeddings for overlapping terms. New (Dutch) terms are subsequently added to the embedding matrix and initialized with the mean of the English embedding matrix.
3. Model is fine-tuned according to the steps in Table A1.

Table A1. Fine-tuning steps of GPT-2. The fastai library was used to split layer groups and to fine-tune the model with one-cycle policy [29]. Differential learning for several layers is applied by passing an array of learning rates `fit_one_cycle()` (https://docs.fast.ai/callback.schedule.html#Learner.fit_one_cycle, accessed on 19 May 2021). Training parameters from Pierre Guillou (https://medium.com/@pierre_guillou/faster-than-training-from-scratch-fine-tuning-the-english-gpt-2-in-any-language-with-hugging-f2ec05c98787, accessed on 19 May 2021).

Step	Layer Groups	Learning Rates
1.	All frozen, fitted for 1 cycle	`fit_one_cycle(1, 2e-3)`
2.	Last two layer groups unfrozen. Fitted for 1 cycle: Decoder blocks 8–11, Vocabulary embedding, Positioning embedding, LayerNorm at model output	`fit_one_cycle(1, slice(1e-3/(2.6**4),1e-3))`
3.	Last three layer groups unfrozen. Fitted for 1 cycle: Previous layers, Decoder blocks 4–7	`fit_one_cycle(1, slice(5e-4/(2.6**4),5e-4))`
4.	All layer groups unfrozen. Fitted for 2 cycles: Previous layers, Decoder blocks 0–3	`fit_one_cycle(2, slice(1e-4/(2.6**4),1e-4))`

Appendix B. Distribution of PHI Tags in Synthetic Corpora

We provide the absolute number of PHI tags per corpus in Table A2 and compare the distribution of tags across corpora in Figure A1. Furthermore, Figure A2 quantifies how much the PHI distribution in each corpus differs from the PHI distribution of the language modeling data (raw numbers for Figure 5).

Table A2. Absolute PHI counts in all corpora. The "LM Corpus" is used to develop the language models. "LM Corpus" counts are reproduced from Table 1 and "NUT" counts from [10].

PHI Tag	LM Corpus	LSTM-p	LSTM-Temp	GPT-p	GPT-Beam	NUT
Name	782,499	20,697	19,839	34,764	6797	9558
Date	202,929	4270	4240	19,879	12,825	3676
Initials	181,811	4038	4166	11,337	2771	778
Address	46,387	1244	1220	6834	299	748
Care Inst.	38,669	1006	985	8537	437	997
Org.	37,284	1091	1041	11,885	1100	712
Location	6977	115	117	1486	56	242
Phone/Fax	3843	45	27	4539	74	97
Age	3350	40	60	416	12	175
Email	2539	40	26	4298	55	95
Hospital	2425	44	46	191	34	92
Profession	537	4	5	32	0	122
URL/IP	326	4	2	723	9	23
ID	232	0	1	200	1	114
Other	105	1	1	0	0	33
SSN	6	0	0	0	0	2
Total	1,309,919	32,639	31,776	105,121	24,470	17,464

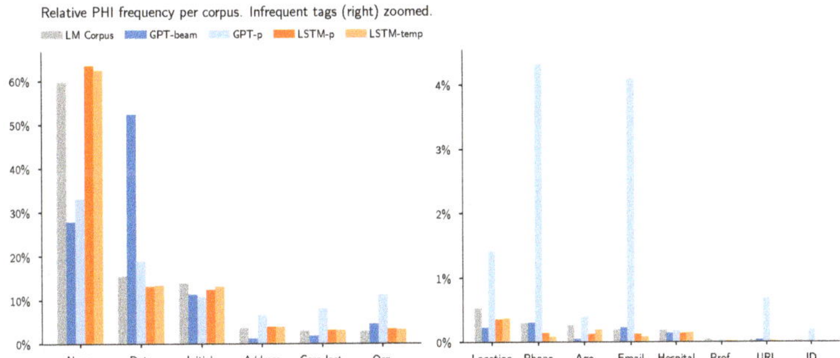

Figure A1. PHI distribution of the synthetic corpora compared to the language modeling corpus.

Raw difference in relative PHI frequency per synthetic corpus compared to the language modeling data.

	GPT-beam	GPT-p	LSTM-p	LSTM-temp
Name	-32 %	-27 %	3.7 %	2.7 %
Date	37 %	3.4 %	-2.4 %	-2.1 %
Initials	-2.6 %	-3.1 %	-1.5 %	-0.77 %
Address	-2.3 %	3 %	0.27 %	0.3 %
Care Institute	-1.2 %	5.2 %	0.13 %	0.15 %
Organization	1.6 %	8.5 %	0.5 %	0.43 %
Internal Location	-0.3 %	0.88 %	-0.18 %	-0.16 %
Phone/Fax	0.01 %	4 %	-0.16 %	-0.21 %
Age	-0.21 %	0.14 %	-0.13 %	-0.07 %
Email	0.03 %	3.9 %	-0.07 %	-0.11 %
Hospital	-0.05 %	-0 %	-0.05 %	-0.04 %
Profession	-0.04 %	-0.01 %	-0.03 %	-0.03 %
URL/IP	0.01 %	0.66 %	-0.01 %	-0.02 %
ID	-0.01 %	0.17 %	-0.02 %	-0.01 %
Other	-0.01 %	-0.01 %	-0 %	-0 %
SSN	-0 %	-0 %	-0 %	-0 %

30 %
20 %
10 %
0 %
-10 %
-20 %
-30 %

Figure A2. Raw increase/decrease in relative PHI frequency per synthetic corpus compared with the PHI distribution of the language modeling corpus. Raw numbers for Figure 5.

Appendix C. Additional Examples of Synthetic Documents

Additional examples for each text generation method are shown in Table A3.

Table A3. Example documents generated by each method with manual English translation. For all examples, we used the same input prompt "Mevr. was vanavond", which translates to "Mrs. was [...] tonight". We transformed <PAR> back into line breaks, but otherwise left in-text annotations as they were generated.

Model	Example (Dutch Original)	Example (English Translation)
LSTM-p	Mevr. was vanavond veel aan het slaan in de huiskamer. Mevr. vertelde dat ze het al even kan laten merken. Op dat moment moest zij even naar het toilet omdat ze kon plassen. Mevr. voelde zich in het inco broekje niet een lange broek aan, ik heb met collega een mail naar de voedingsadministratie gedaan.	Mrs. was beating much in the living room tonight. Mrs. told that she could let notice it already. At that moment she had to go the toilet because she could pee. Mrs. felt herself in the inco pants not long pants wearing, I have send an email to the food administration with a colleague.
LSTM-temp	Mevr. was vanavond niet op de Huismus. Moest het haar nog een keertje uit zetten. Ik heb mevr. haar appartement laten zien en met 2 poten op de stoel gelopen. Mevr. heeft niet veel geslapen. Mevr. heeft vannacht niet verschoond en deze ging nu altijd bij, zat prima in haar stoel.	Mrs. was not at the Huismus tonight. Had to turn her off for once. I showed mrs. her apartment and walked with 2 legs at the chair. Mrs. has not slept much. Mrs. did not change tonight and this now always went with, sat in her chair fine.
GPT-p	Mevr. was vanavond rustig aanwezig. Mw. heeft vanavond goed gegeten en gedronken. <NameSTART> Lucy <NameEND> Rapp. <NameSTART> B. Greenwood <NameEND> broecks Dag <NameSTART> Barbara <NameEND>, Ik heb net contact gehad met <NameSTART> Alex <NameEND>. <Organization_CompanySTART> de Zonnebloem <Organization_CompanyEND> <NameSTART> Jane <NameEND> is op de hoogte van de situatie.	Mrs. was quietly present tonight. Mrs. has eaten and drank well tonight. <NameSTART> Lucy <NameEND> Rep. <NameSTART> B. Greenwood <NameEND> broecks Hello <NameSTART> Barbara <NameEND>, I have just had contact with <NameSTART> Alex <NameEND>. <Organization_CompanySTART> de Zonnebloem <Organization_CompanyEND> <NameSTART> Jane <NameEND> is aware of the situation.
GPT-beam	Mevr. was vanavond rustig aanwezig. Mevr. heeft goed gegeten en gedronken. Mevr. is om 21.00 uur naar bed geholpen. mevr. gaf aan erg moe te zijn en graag naar bed te willen. Mevr. is om 22.30 uur in bed geholpen en ligt tot nu toe nog te slapen. <DateSTART> Zondag <DateEND> komt mevr. weer naar de dagbesteding. <unk> Mevr. geeft aan het erg naar haar zin te hebben gehad.	Mrs. was quietly present tonight. Mrs. has eaten and drank well. Mrs. was helped to bed at 9 pm. Mrs. indicated to be very tired and would like to go to bed. Mrs. was helped to bed at 10.30 pm and is still sleeping until now. <DateSTART> Sunday <DateEND> mrs. will come to the daytime activities. Mrs. indicated that she had a great time.

Appendix D. Privacy User Study: Annotation Guidelines and Data Sampling

We provide annotation guidelines in Figure A4. Below, we outline the steps to filter a sample of real-synthetic document pairs SR for presentation to participants. We denote a synthetic document as $s \in S$ and a real document as $r \in R$.

1. Remove duplicates: for the same document s, ROUGE-3 and ROUGE-5 may retrieve the same document r.
2. Sort the synthetic documents by ROUGE-3 and ROUGE-5 recall and keep the top-100 of both lists. (The top 100 ROUGE-3 recall scores were between 0.18 and 1.0 with an average of 0.307 and a median of 0.233. The top 100 ROUGE-5 recall scores were between 0.111 and 1.0 with an average of 0.236 and a median of 0.164.) The idea is that we investigate high risk documents with highly similar counterparts among the real data. Add these documents to SR.
3. For the remaining documents in SR, retrieve the most similar document with BM25.
4. Remove documents longer than 1000 characters to control annotation effort.

5. Remove documents that had a high overlap due to structural elements (e.g., <PAR> token or punctuation).

Appendix E. Evaluating the Impact of the Synthetic Dataset Size

The effectiveness of a downstream machine learning method necessarily depends on the number of (synthetic) training examples. For simplicity, we fixed the size of the synthetic datasets across all our experiments (cf. Section 3.3.3). To analyze if it would be beneficial to increase/decrease the size of the synthetic corpora, we trained de-identification models on subsets of the data. Figure A3 shows the entity-level F1-score for varying training set sizes. We find that the learning curve flattens at around 70% of the training data, indicating that there is little benefit to generate even larger synthetic corpora. Due to computational constraints, we limited this experiment to one synthetic corpus (LSTM-p).

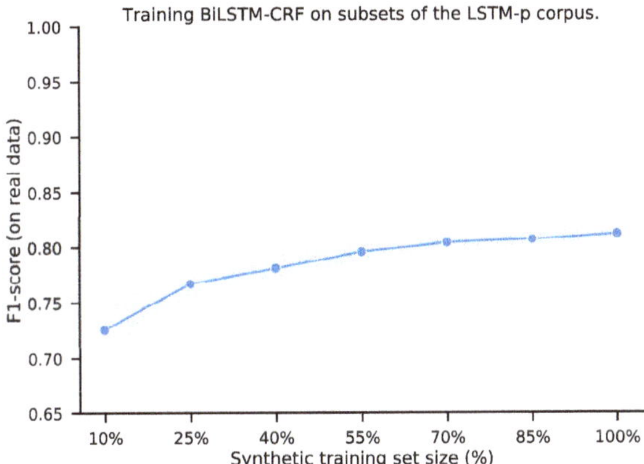

Figure A3. Entity-level F1-score for varying LSTM-p training set sizes. The full training set (100%) consists of all training and validation documents in LSTM-p. The F1-score is measured on the *NUT* test set. For each subset size, we train/test each model 3 times. The line shows the averaged scores along with the 95% confidence interval.

User Study: Synthetic Text Privacy

This research aims to create synthetic text data using a machine learning model trained on real patient data. While this synthetic text is meant to share properties with the realdata to be of use in further research, it should not contain information from the real data that could help re-identifying people contained in the real dataset. For example you could ask: If I was a patient mentioned in the real dataset, could one learn something about me by looking at the synthetic data?
Differently to structured datasets with clearly defined attributes (Name, Date, Diagnosis...), free text data is more complicated and harder to evaluate, as privacy sensitive information can be disclosed via context or different phrasing. As machine-calculated similarity scores are not very indicative of privacy breaches, it is necessary to have a human evaluate some examples, especially because there is not always a right or wrong answer.

Data: During the evaluation, you will get (1) a synthetic piece of text and (2) a similar text from the real dataset, which we present as potential source document for the given synthetic text. There are no true 1:1 matches between original and fake texts, so you may get to see the same synthetic text twice, but with different potential source texts.

Questions: You will be asked the same questions for each example. The aim is to better understand whether privacy of people in the real dataset is compromised by looking at the synthetic data. Note that we do NOT care about how realistic/grammatical the synthetic texts are. Please read each text carefully. It is up to you to decide whether you consider certain information as privacy sensitive, as there is no right or wrong answer.

For any questions or feedback, please contact me on Slack @claudia.libbi

Ethical Approval

We did a DPIA (Data Protection Impact Assessment) with the Privacy Officer at Nedap.
The data that will be shown to you is privacy sensitive and may be used within this research project and can not be shared with any third person.

I understand that I may not share this data with anyone else.

Confidentiality

Your answers will be treated confidentially and stored anonymously for the duration of this study, as we do not need to re-identify you as evaluator after data collection.
Your name will not be mentioned in any publications resulting from this research unless you explicitly consent to this.

I understand that my answers will be treated confidentially and will be stored anonymously for the duration of this research.

Next

Figure A4. Annotation guidelines for the privacy user study.

References

1. Wang, Y.; Wang, L.; Rastegar-Mojarad, M.; Moon, S.; Shen, F.; Afzal, N.; Liu, S.; Zeng, Y.; Mehrabi, S.; Sohn, S.; et al. Clinical information extraction applications: A literature review. *J. Biomed. Inform.* **2018**, *77*, 34–49. [CrossRef] [PubMed]
2. Bellovin, S.M.; Dutta, P.K.; Reitinger, N. Privacy and synthetic datasets. *Stan. Tech. L Rev.* **2019**, *22*, 1. [CrossRef]
3. Rankin, D.; Black, M.; Bond, R.; Wallace, J.; Mulvenna, M.; Epelde, G. Reliability of supervised machine learning using synthetic data in health care: Model to preserve privacy for data sharing. *JMIR Med. Inform.* **2020**, *8*, e18910. [CrossRef] [PubMed]
4. Wang, L.; Liu, J.; Liu, J. Investigating Label Bias in Beam Search for Open-ended Text Generation. *arXiv* **2020**, arXiv:2005.11009.
5. El Emam, K.; Mosquera, L.; Bass, J. Evaluating Identity Disclosure Risk in Fully Synthetic Health Data: Model Development and Validation. *J. Med. Internet Res.* **2020**, *22*, e23139. [CrossRef] [PubMed]
6. Radford, A.; Wu, J.; Child, R.; Luan, D.; Amodei, D.; Sutskever, I. Language models are unsupervised multitask learners. *OpenAI Blog* **2019**, *1*, 9.
7. Melamud, O.; Shivade, C. Towards Automatic Generation of Shareable Synthetic Clinical Notes Using Neural Language Models. In Proceedings of the 2nd Clinical Natural Language Processing Workshop, Minneapolis, MN, USA, 7 June 2019; pp. 35–45.
8. Amin-Nejad, A.; Ive, J.; Velupillai, S. Exploring Transformer Text Generation for Medical Dataset Augmentation. In Proceedings of the 12th Language Resources and Evaluation Conference, LREC Marseille, France, 11–16 May 2020; pp. 4699–4708.

9. Meystre, S.M. De-identification of Unstructured Clinical Data for Patient Privacy Protection. In *Medical Data Privacy Handbook*; Gkoulalas-Divanis, A., Loukides, G., Eds.; Springer International Publishing: Berlin/Heidelberg, Germany, 2015; pp. 697–716.
10. Trienes, J.; Trieschnigg, D.; Seifert, C.; Hiemstra, D. Comparing Rule-based, Feature-based and Deep Neural Methods for De-identification of Dutch Medical Records. In Proceedings of the ACM WSDM 2020 Health Search and Data Mining Workshop, co-located with the 13th ACM International WSDM Conference, HSDM@WSDM 2020, Houston, TX, USA, 6–9 February 2020; Volume 2551, pp. 3–11.
11. Lin, C.Y. ROUGE: A Package for Automatic Evaluation of Summaries. In *Text Summarization Branches Out*; Association for Computational Linguistics: Barcelona, Spain, 2004; pp. 74–81.
12. Manning, C.D.; Raghavan, P.; Schütze, H. *Introduction to Information Retrieval*; Cambridge University Press: Cambridge, UK, 2008.
13. Liu, P.J. Learning to Write Notes in Electronic Health Records. *arXiv* **2018**, arXiv:1808.02622.
14. Wang, Z.; Ive, J.; Velupillai, S.; Specia, L. Is artificial data useful for biomedical Natural Language Processing algorithms? In Proceedings of the 18th BioNLP Workshop and Shared Task, BioNLP@ACL 2019, Florence, Italy, 1 August 2019; pp. 240–249.
15. Ive, J.; Viani, N.; Kam, J.; Yin, L.; Verma, S.; Puntis, S.; Cardinal, R.N.; Roberts, A.; Stewart, R.; Velupillai, S. Generation and evaluation of artificial mental health records for Natural Language Processing. *NPJ Digit. Med.* **2020**, *3*, 1–9. [CrossRef] [PubMed]
16. de Vries, W.; van Cranenburgh, A.; Bisazza, A.; Caselli, T.; van Noord, G.; Nissim, M. BERTje: A Dutch BERT Model. *arXiv* **2019**, arXiv:1912.09582.
17. Delobelle, P.; Winters, T.; Berendt, B. RobBERT: A Dutch RoBERTa-based Language Model. In Proceedings of the 2020 Conference on Empirical Methods in Natural Language Processing: Findings, EMNLP 2020, Online Event, 16–20 November 2020; pp. 3255–3265.
18. Peng, N.; Ghazvininejad, M.; May, J.; Knight, K. Towards Controllable Story Generation. In Proceedings of the First Workshop on Storytelling, Grenoble, France, 26 March 2018; pp. 43–49.
19. Yoon, J. End-to-End Machine Learning Frameworks for Medicine: Data Imputation, Model Interpretation and Synthetic Data Generation. Ph.D. Thesis, UCLA, Shenzhen, China, 2020.
20. Hochreiter, S.; Schmidhuber, J. Long Short-Term Memory. *Neural Comput.* **1997**, *9*, 1735–1780. [CrossRef] [PubMed]
21. Vaswani, A.; Shazeer, N.; Parmar, N.; Uszkoreit, J.; Jones, L.; Gomez, A.N.; Kaiser, L.; Polosukhin, I. Attention is All you Need. In Proceedings of the Advances in Neural Information Processing Systems 30: Annual Conference on Neural Information Processing Systems 2017, Long Beach, CA, USA, 4–9 December 2017; pp. 5998–6008.
22. Zoph, B.; Yuret, D.; May, J.; Knight, K. Transfer Learning for Low-Resource Neural Machine Translation. In Proceedings of the 2016 Conference on Empirical Methods in Natural Language Processing, EMNLP 2016, Austin, TX, USA, 1–5 November 2016; pp. 1568–1575.
23. Mattei, L.D.; Cafagna, M.; Dell'Orletta, F.; Nissim, M.; Guerini, M. GePpeTto Carves Italian into a Language Model. In Proceedings of the Seventh Italian Conference on Computational Linguistics, CLiC-it 2020, Bologna, Italy, 1–3 March 2020; Volume 2769.
24. Holtzman, A.; Buys, J.; Du, L.; Forbes, M.; Choi, Y. The Curious Case of Neural Text Degeneration. In Proceedings of the 8th International Conference on Learning Representations, ICLR 2020, Addis Ababa, Ethiopia, 26–30 April 2020.
25. Nadeem, M.; He, T.; Cho, K.; Glass, J. A Systematic Characterization of Sampling Algorithms for Open-ended Language Generation. In Proceedings of the 1st Conference of the Asia-Pacific Chapter of the Association for Computational Linguistics and the 10th International Joint Conference on Natural Language Processing, Online, 17–18 October 2020; pp. 334–346.
26. Welleck, S.; Kulikov, I.; Roller, S.; Dinan, E.; Cho, K.; Weston, J. Neural Text Generation With Unlikelihood Training. In Proceedings of the 8th International Conference on Learning Representations, ICLR 2020, Addis Ababa, Ethiopia, 26–30 April 2020.
27. Stubbs, A.; Uzuner, Ö.; Kotfila, C.; Goldstein, I.; Szolovits, P. Challenges in Synthesizing Surrogate PHI in Narrative EMRs. In *Medical Data Privacy Handbook*; Gkoulalas-Divanis, A., Loukides, G., Eds.; Springer International Publishing: Berlin/Heidelberg, Germany, 2015; pp. 717–735.
28. de Vries, W.; Nissim, M. As Good as New. How to Successfully Recycle English GPT-2 to Make Models for Other Languages. *arXiv* **2020**, arXiv:2012.05628.
29. Smith, L.N.; Topin, N. Super-Convergence: Very Fast Training of Neural Networks Using Large Learning Rates. *arXiv* **2018**, arXiv:1708.07120.
30. Menger, V.; Scheepers, F.; van Wijk, L.M.; Spruit, M. DEDUCE: A pattern matching method for automatic de-identification of Dutch medical text. *Telemat. Inform.* **2018**, *35*, 727–736. [CrossRef]
31. Choi, E.; Biswal, S.; Malin, B.A.; Duke, J.; Stewart, W.F.; Sun, J. Generating Multi-label Discrete Patient Records using Generative Adversarial Networks. In Proceedings of the Machine Learning for Health Care Conference, MLHC 2017, Boston, MA, USA, 18–19 August 2017; Volume 68, pp. 286–305.
32. Keskar, N.S.; McCann, B.; Varshney, L.R.; Xiong, C.; Socher, R. CTRL: A Conditional Transformer Language Model for Controllable Generation. *arXiv* **2019**, arXiv:1909.05858.
33. Dathathri, S.; Madotto, A.; Lan, J.; Hung, J.; Frank, E.; Molino, P.; Yosinski, J.; Liu, R. Plug and Play Language Models: A Simple Approach to Controlled Text Generation. In Proceedings of the 8th International Conference on Learning Representations, ICLR 2020, Addis Ababa, Ethiopia, 26–30 April 2020.

34. HIPAA. Guidance Regarding Methods for De-Identification of Protected Health Information in Accordance with the Health Insurance Portability and Accountability Act (HIPAA) Privacy Rule. Available online: https://www.hhs.gov/hipaa/for-professionals/privacy/special-topics/de-identification/index.html (accessed on 19 May 2021).
35. Hittmeir, M.; Ekelhart, A.; Mayer, R. Utility and Privacy Assessments of Synthetic Data for Regression Tasks. In Proceedings of the 2019 IEEE International Conference on Big Data (Big Data), Los Angeles, CA, USA, 9–12 December 2019; pp. 5763–5772.

future internet

Article

A Classification Method for Academic Resources Based on a Graph Attention Network

Jie Yu *, Yaliu Li, Chenle Pan and Junwei Wang

School of Computer Engineering and Science, Shanghai University, Shanghai 200444, China; yabobo@shu.edu.cn (Y.L.); panchenle08@shu.edu.cn (C.P.); jun121@shu.edu.cn (J.Y.)
* Correspondence: jieyu@shu.edu.cn

Abstract: Classification of resource can help us effectively reduce the work of filtering massive academic resources, such as selecting relevant papers and focusing on the latest research by scholars in the same field. However, existing graph neural networks do not take into account the associations between academic resources, leading to unsatisfactory classification results. In this paper, we propose an Association Content Graph Attention Network (ACGAT), which is based on the association features and content attributes of academic resources. The semantic relevance and academic relevance are introduced into the model. The ACGAT makes full use of the association commonality and the influence information of resources and introduces an attention mechanism to improve the accuracy of academic resource classification. We conducted experiments on a self-built scholar network and two public citation networks. Experimental results show that the ACGAT has better effectiveness than existing classification methods.

Keywords: academic resource; attention; association features; content attributes; classification

Citation: Yu, J.; Li, Y.; Pan, C.; Wang, J. A Classification Method for Academic Resources Based on a Graph Attention Network. *Future Internet* **2021**, *13*, 64. https://doi.org/10.3390/fi13030064

Academic Editor: Massimo Esposito

Received: 5 February 2021
Accepted: 2 March 2021
Published: 4 March 2021

1. Introduction

With the rapid development of the internet, we have entered the era of big data [1]. In the academic field, scientific research has been supported and a large number of academic resources have been generated with the development of science and technology. Academic resources include a large number of academic research papers, academic researchers, and all the information that can be mined, such as an author's research field and activities. Faced with the rapid growth of information resources, it is difficult for users to filter information. Academic resources are different from general information resources [2]. On the one hand, there is a wide range of information sources, and information is freely released. On the other hand, there are many and diverse types of academic resources. Therefore, it is particularly important to classify academic resources quickly and effectively [3]. At the same time, as an important means of resource organization and management, information classification [4] can effectively integrate academic resources and easily realize information retrieval, which is also the premise and foundation of personalized recommendation.

However, existing graph neural networks still have some limitations in the classification of academic resources. They ignore the influence information of the academic resources and allocate the neighborhood aggregation coefficient uniformly. Furthermore, they only use the connectivity and do not fully utilize the association information of edges, such as the strength and type [5]. As a result, the deviation of information aggregation in an academic resource network affects the accuracy of classification. In order to cope with the challenges above, this paper proposes an Association Content Graph Attention Network (ACGAT), which is based on association features and content attributes in order to classify academic resources. First, on the one hand, the model mines the association commonality among academic resource nodes to improve the aggregation of the network by reducing the existence of isolated nodes in the existing graph attention network. On the other hand, the model calculates the influence of a node, which enhances the positive effect of the node on the network and weakens the negative impact of the isolated nodes. Then, the content attributes of academic resources are extracted to mine the semantic similarity of nodes, which enriches the content of nodes. Finally, the model integrates the acquired information of academic relevance and semantic relevance from two dimensions. The attention mechanism is used to update the features of academic resources. The ACGAT can improve the accuracy of the classification of academic resources, including the types of papers and the research fields of the scholars. In addition, it can also classify other social networks that can mine edge information.

2. Related Work

Graph data contain two types of information: attribute information [6] and structure information [7]. Attribute information describes the inherent properties of objects in a graph, and structure information describes the information on associations between objects. The structure generated by associations is not only helpful for the description of nodes in graph data, but also plays a key role in the description of the whole graph. It is a key challenge in graph learning to effectively learn the complex non-Euclidean structure of graph data. The existing graph-embedding methods aim to learn the low-dimensional potential representations of nodes in a network [8]. The learned feature representation can be used as a feature in various graph-based tasks, such as classification, clustering, and link prediction. The traditional methods of realizing graph learning are mainly divided into two categories. One is comprised of embedding methods based on matrix decomposition, such as the graph factorization (GF) algorithm [9] and GraRep [10]. The other is based on a random walk, such as DeepWalk [11], LINE [12], and node2vec [13]. However, the embedding of traditional graph learning cannot capture complex patterns and does not incorporate node features, resulting in low-accuracy node classification results.

A graph neural network (GNN) [14] is a kind of neural network model that can operate on graph structure data to convey graph information. It uses the node information and structure information of a graph to effectively mine the information contained in the graph data. GNNs have achieved excellent results in many application fields, such as image recognition [15] and heterogeneous graph learning [16]. Convolution operations have been extended to graph learning with graph convolution networks (GCNs) [17]. Niepert et al. [18] proposed a convolution method that was applied to a graph data model, which needed to sort graph nodes and had high complexity. Kipf et al. [19] mapped graph features in the time domain to the spectral frequency domain and approximately simplified them with Chebyshev polynomials, which achieved successful results in semi-supervised classification of graph nodes. In addition to graph convolution networks, many researchers have introduced attention mechanisms to implement graph node classification. Petar [20] first proposed a graph attention network (GAT) that assigned different weights to different nodes in the neighborhood. Gong and Cheng [5] added edge feature vectors directly, which extended the attention mechanism proposed for the first time and focused on each type of feature neighborhood. Gilmer et al. [21] introduced an edge network in which the eigenvectors of edges were used as input and output matrices to transform the embedding of adjacent nodes. Lu et al. [22] proposed a channel graph attention network based on edge content, which could find the fine-grained signals of node interaction from text information and improve the accuracy of node characterization. The classification results of graph nodes show that the adaptive ability of GATs makes them more effective in fusing the information of node features and graph topology.

In existing research, it was effective to combine edge content in information aggregation. However, the feature content on the edge of the connections, such as intensity, has not been fully explored. In the classification of academic resources, ignoring the rich information on associations between resource nodes will lead to unsatisfactory classification results. Therefore, in this paper, we use semantic relevance and academic relevance (commonality between resources and influence information) for information aggregation to effectively improve the classification accuracy of academic resource network nodes.

3. Definition

3.1. Definition of Notations

We define the academic resource network as an undirected graph $G = (V, E)$, where V is the node set, and $|V| = N$ is the number of nodes. The feature vector of a set of nodes can be expressed as $h = \{h_1, h_2, \ldots, h_N\}, \quad h_i \in \mathbb{R}^F$. The feature vector is generated by keywords of statistical academic resources, where F is the dimension of the node features. The size of matrix h is $N * F$, which represents the features of all nodes in the graph, and each node is represented by a word vector of dimension F. Each element of the word vector corresponds to a word, and the element has only two values of 0 (nonexistence) or 1 (existence). E is a set of edges that indicates the connectivity between nodes. The aggregation coefficients involved in the aggregation process are the academic association commonality coefficient e_{ij}, association influence coefficient β_{ij}, and semantic similarity coefficient α_{ij}. We define a minimal set of definitions required to understand this paper in Table 1.

Table 1. Commonly used notations.

Notations	Descriptions
G	A graph.
V	The set of nodes in a graph.
v_i	A node $v_i \in V$.
E	The set of edges in a graph.
N	The number of nodes, $N = \|V\|$.
$h \in \mathbb{R}^F$	The feature vector of a set of nodes.
F	The dimension of the node features.
q_{ij}	The academic association commonality coefficient.
e_{ij}	The weighted coefficients of the association commonality.
λ_{ij}	The association influence coefficient.
α_{ij}	The semantic similarity coefficient.
A	The influence factor matrix.
D	The degree matrix, D.
$d_{(v_i)}$	The degree of node v_i.
M	The number of neighbors of a node v.
θ	The shared attention mechanism.
N_v	The neighbors of a node v.
W	The sharing parameter.
$[\cdot \|\| \cdot]$	Splicing operation.
W_ε, W_e, W_D	Learning parameters, including the academic semantic relevance, academic association commonality, and influence coefficient.
λ_{ij}	The final coefficient.
$\sigma(\cdot)$	The activation function.
K	The multi-attention number.

3.2. Academic Resource Networks

In the construction of academic resource networks, this paper constructs a cooperation network based on the cooperative relationships between scholars and a citation network based on the citation relationship between papers. In the cooperation network, v_i represents an author, the node feature F is described by the keywords extracted from the author's published papers as the content attributes of the node, and the association information on the edge indicates the cooperation relationships between authors. In the citation network, v_i stands for a paper. The keywords of the papers are used as content attributes to represent the feature F of the node. The edge indicates that there is a citation relationship between papers. We provide two simple examples of a scholar cooperation network (Figure 1a) and a citation network (Figure 1b).

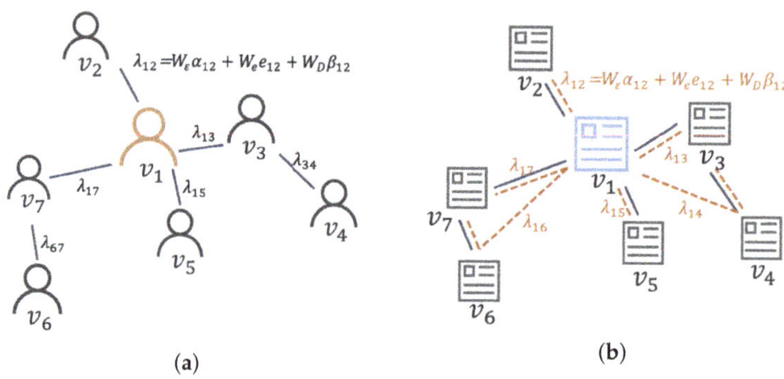

Figure 1. (**a**) Scholar cooperation network. (**b**) Citation network.

In the scholar cooperation network, nodes represent scholars, and the edges between nodes represent the cooperative relationships between scholars. The final aggregation coefficient λ_{ij} is determined by the semantic similarity coefficient α_{ij}, association influence coefficient β_{ij}, and weighted coefficients of the association community e_{ij}. In the citation network, nodes represent papers, and the edges between nodes represent the citation relationships between papers. The black solid line represents the actual reference relationship, and the red dotted line represents the built reference relationship. Similarly, the final aggregation coefficient λ_{ij} is also composed of three coefficients.

4. Proposed Method

We propose an Association Content Graph Attention Network (ACGAT) based on association features and content attributes to classify academic resources. Semantic association and academic association are introduced into the model. Firstly, the discrete academic resources are integrated into an academic resource network by using the association commonality and influence information between resources through a transformation operation. Then, an attention mechanism [23] is used to aggregate the neighborhood information to obtain the final node features to improve the accuracy of academic resource classification. The overall framework is shown in Figure 2.

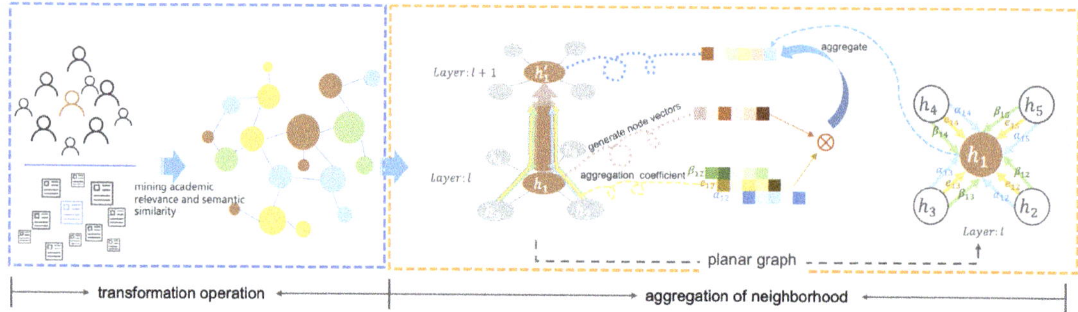

Figure 2. Diagram of the overall framework of the Association Content Graph Attention Network (ACGAT). The left part is the transformation operation, which transforms the discrete points into the resource graph structure. The right part is the aggregation operation, which aggregates the domain information and uses the final aggregation coefficient λ_{ij} to get the new feature representation of the central node.

4.1. Mining and Representation of Academic Relevance

Academic relevance includes the influence information and the commonality between resources. Inspired by PageRank [24], the influence of the node is of great significance for the aggregation of information of neighboring nodes. However, the existing model does not consider the influence factor. In collaborative networks, the author weight represents the degree of activity of authors in a certain research field. In citation networks, node weights represent the academic relevance and influence in the networks. Thus, the ACGAT introduces the influence factor of the node, thus enhancing the positive effect of the node on the network and weakening the possible negative effects of isolated nodes.

The calculation method for the influence factor matrix A is as follows:

- We calculate the degree matrix D of a network of N nodes, where $d_{(v_i)}$ is the degree of node v_i.

$$D = \begin{pmatrix} d_{(v_1)} & 0 & \cdots & 0 \\ 0 & d_{(v_2)} & \cdots & 0 \\ \vdots & \vdots & \ddots & \vdots \\ 0 & 0 & \cdots & d_{(v_N)} \end{pmatrix}$$

- The influence D_{ij} of neighboring node j on central node i is expressed as the ratio of the degree of node j to the degree of node i, which can be obtained according to Equation (1).
- The influence factor β_{ij} of each node and $A = \begin{pmatrix} \beta_{11} & \beta_{12} & \cdots & \beta_{1N} \\ \beta_{21} & \beta_{22} & \cdots & \beta_{2N} \\ \vdots & \vdots & \ddots & \vdots \\ \beta_{N1} & \beta_{N2} & \cdots & \beta_{NN} \end{pmatrix}$ are obtained through normalization according to Equation (2).

$$D_{ij} = \frac{d_j}{d_i} \tag{1}$$

$$\beta_{ij} = \frac{D_{ij}}{\sum_m^M D_{im}} \tag{2}$$

D_{ij} is the influence of node j on node i. In the author cooperation network, D_{ij} is the ratio of the number of collaborators of author j to that of author i. In the citation network, D_{ij} is the ratio of the number of citation associations of paper j to that of paper i. β_{ij} is the influence factor of the normalized final node j on node i.

In this paper, we not only introduce the influence of academic resource nodes, but also integrate the association commonality between nodes into the model. In the citation network, the citation relationship between papers is a sparse matrix. We refer to the network-embedded model LINE [12], which not only obtains the local similarity of two nodes in the network, but also retains the second-order similarity between a pair of nodes (u, v), that is, the similarity of their adjacent network structures. Citation networks have not only first-order similarity in content, but also second-order similarity in structure [25]. If the second-order similarity is high, there are no direct citation relationships, but there are a large number of co-cited relationships between papers. The higher the correlation, the more similar the two papers are. As shown in Figure 3, the relationship between paper 6 and paper 7 is a first-order local similarity, while the relationship between paper 5 and paper 6 belongs to second-order global similarity because they have the same co-citations, but no direct reference relationship. Based on this, when we construct the correlation matrix in the citation network, we are not limited to the information of directly related papers. We consider the papers that are adjacent and similar in structure, but have no real citation relationships. The shortest path [26] between nodes can exactly reflect the structural relationships between authors. We calculate the shortest path between nodes in the citation network as the association information between nodes. According to Equation (3), we get the coefficient q_{ij} as the coefficient of association commonality between two nodes in the citation network. q_{ij} is positively correlated with the degree of association and the commonality between two papers.

$$q_{ij} = \frac{1}{dis_{ij}} \tag{3}$$

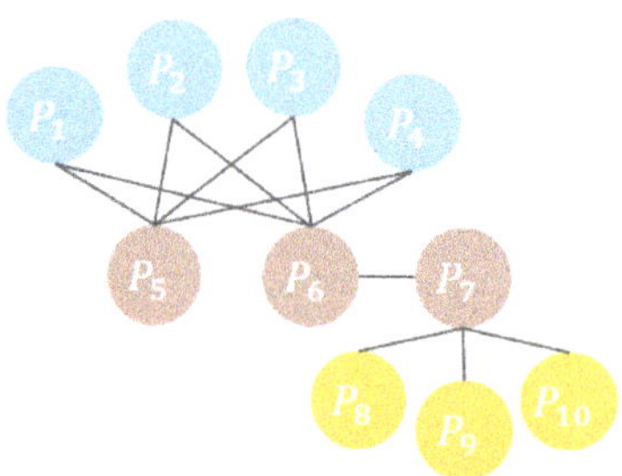

Figure 3. Diagram of second-order relationships between resources.

Similarly, in the author cooperation network, nodes represent scholars and the connecting edges indicate that there is cooperation between authors. When the number of papers co-authored by two authors is larger, it means that the collaboration between the authors is closer, the commonality between the authors is greater, and the research fields are more related. As shown in Figure 4, author A has published six papers with author B, and author A has published three papers with author C. Obviously, the cooperation intensity between A and B is higher than with of other collaborators. Therefore, we introduce the cooperation strength into the scholar network as the association coefficient q_{ij} of the nodes in the model.

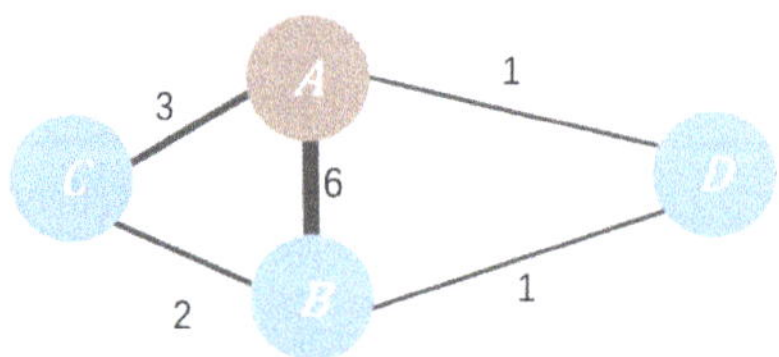

Figure 4. Schematic diagram of scholar cooperation. The number between scholars indicates the number of articles written in collaboration.

Existing graph neural networks have a drawback in the representation of academic resource relationships, that is, the adjacency matrix belongs to a binary matrix (0 or 1), which can only indicate the existence of connectivity between nodes. However, the connection edge in the graph of an academic resource network contains rich information, such as strength and type, which is not a binary index variable. Therefore, the ACGAT combines the common association features of the edges and normalizes them in a bidirectional manner. We obtain the weighted coefficients e_{ij} of the association commonality between nodes i and j according to the Equation (4):

$$e_{ij} = \frac{q_{ij}}{\sum_{m=1}^{M} q_{im}}, \tag{4}$$

where M is the number of neighbor nodes of the central node. In the citation network, M represents the number of papers related to paper i in the association graph constructed above, and q_{ij} represents the reciprocal of the shortest path between papers. In the author cooperation network, M represents the number of authors who have cooperative relationships with author i, and q_{ij} represents the intensity of paper cooperation between authors.

After obtaining the weighted coefficient of correlation commonality, we transform the original binary adjacency graph (Figure 5a) into a bidirectional edge feature graph (Figure 5b) about the central node i, which is not a symmetric matrix and retains more abundant academic resource information.

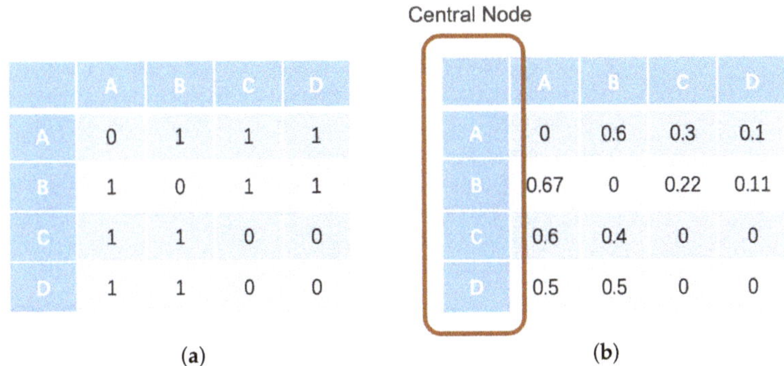

	A	B	C	D
A	0	1	1	1
B	1	0	1	1
C	1	1	0	0
D	1	1	0	0

(a)

Central Node

	A	B	C	D
A	0	0.6	0.3	0.1
B	0.67	0	0.22	0.11
C	0.6	0.4	0	0
D	0.5	0.5	0	0

(b)

Figure 5. Adjacency feature graph. (**a**) Original binary adjacency graph; (**b**) an asymmetric bidirectional edge feature graph of the central node.

4.2. Aggregation Based on an Attention Mechanism

In the application of academic resources, existing graph attention networks only calculate the attention based on the semantic similarity of nodes, but often neglect association information between academic resource nodes. The ACGAT introduces the semantic relevance and academic relevance of academic resources into the model and integrates them. In the process of the dissemination of information of graph nodes, it is necessary to learn three distribution parameters, which are the semantic similarity, association commonality, and influence information. According to these three parameters, we get the final updated feature of the aggregated attention coefficient and classify the academic resource nodes to improve the accuracy.

The ACGAT takes the semantic feature $h = \{h_1, h_2, \ldots, h_N\}, \quad h_i \in \mathbb{R}^F$ of the academic resource node as input, and all of the node features will be transformed by the linear change matrix Wg. A shared attention mechanism θ is used on the node to calculate the measurement of similarity between nodes according to the features of the input nodes. Similarly to the graph attention model [20], this model calculates the measurement of similarity between the adjacent node and the center node using Equation (5):

$$\varepsilon_{ij} = \theta\left(\left[Wh_i || Wh_j\right]\right), j \in \mathcal{N}_i, \tag{5}$$

where $\mathcal{N}_i$ is the neighbor collection of node i. First, a linear-mapping sharing parameter W is used to increase the dimensions of the vertex features. Then, $[\cdot||\cdot]$ splices the transformed features of vertices i and j. Finally, $\theta(\cdot)$ maps the spliced high-dimensional features to a real number.

The similarity measurement of the content features is normalized by the $softmax$ function [27] of Equation (6) to obtain the attention coefficient α_{ij} of the academic semantic features.

$$\alpha_{ij} = softmax(\varepsilon_{ij}) = \frac{\exp(\varepsilon_{ij})}{\sum_{k \in \mathcal{N}_i} \exp(\varepsilon_{ik})} \tag{6}$$

The advantage of using *LeakyReLU* is that in the process of back propagation, the gradient can also be calculated for parts of the input of *LeakyReLU* activation function that are less than zero [28]. The factor calculated by the attention mechanism is obtained using Equation (7).

$$\alpha_{ij} = softmax(\varepsilon_{ij}) = \frac{\exp(LeakyReLU(\theta[Wh_i \| Wh_j]))}{\sum_{k \in \mathcal{N}_i} \exp(LeakyReLU(\theta[Wh_i \| Wh_k]))} \quad (7)$$

Then, the aggregation coefficient is obtained as shown in Equation (8):

$$\lambda_{ij} = W_{\varepsilon}\alpha_{ij} + W_e e_{ij} + W_D \beta_{ij}, \quad (8)$$

where W_{ε}, W_e, and W_D are learning parameters that reflect the influence of three dimensions of academic semantic similarity, including academic semantic relevance, academic association commonality, and the influence coefficient. λ_{ij} is the coefficient of the final fusion of academic resources.

The final aggregate attention coefficient is used to calculate the linear combinations of related features. The result is the final output of each node, and $\sigma(\cdot)$ is the activation function, as shown in Equation (9).

$$h'_i = \sigma\left(\sum_{j \in \mathcal{N}_i} \lambda_{ij} W h_j\right) \quad (9)$$

According to the existing multiple-attention mechanism [29], K independent attention mechanisms are used to execute Equation (9), and their features are related. The essence of multiple heads is the calculation of multiple independent attentions, which acts as an integrated function to prevent over-fitting. In the last layer of the neural network, the output feature expression of the result is updated, resulting in Equation (10).

$$h'_i = \sigma\left(\frac{1}{K}\sum_{k=1}^{K}\sum_{j \in \mathcal{N}_i} \lambda_{ij}^k W^k h_j\right) \quad (10)$$

5. Experiment

In order to verify the feasibility of the ACGAT, we conducted comparative experiments on a self-built dataset and two public datasets. The following two sub-sections will introduce the datasets and analyze the results.

5.1. Datasets

In this paper, we used a self-built scholar cooperative network dataset, SIG, and the public citation network datasets Cora and Citeseer [30] to verify the classification effect of our model on academic resources. The basic situations of these three data networks are as follows.

SIG is composed of research scholars of special interest groups on the ACM website, including information retrieval (IR), the Ada programming language (DA), information technology education (ITE), computer graphics (GRAPH), accessibility and computing (ACCESS), bioinformatics and computational biology (BIO), knowledge discovery in data (KDD), and artificial intelligence (AI)—a total of eight categories. We selected 3669 scholars who published at least four papers in various fields for research. According to their published academic papers, we obtained the cooperation relationships between scholars, selected the keywords with word frequencies greater than 10 as the feature dimension, and constructed a scholar cooperation network. The scholar cooperation network contained 3669 nodes and 10,399 edges, and each node had 3664 feature dimensions.

Cora is composed of machine learning papers, which are divided into seven categories: case-based, genetic algorithms, neural networks, probabilistic methods, reinforcement learning, rule learning, and theory. In the final corpus, each paper was cited by at least one other paper. There were 2708 papers in the whole corpus. There were 2708 nodes and

5429 edges in the citation network of the Cora dataset, and each node had 1433 feature dimensions.

Citeseer contains 3312 scientific publications, which are divided into six categories: agents, artificial intelligence (AI), database (DB), information retrieval (IR), machine learning (ML), and human–computer interaction (HCI). The dataset contains 3312 nodes and 4732 edges, and each node has 3708 feature dimensions.

The specific information of the three datasets is shown in Table 2.

Table 2. Summary of the datasets.

Datasets		Nodes	Edges	Features	Classes
Scholar cooperation network	SIG	3669	10,399	3664	8
Citation network	Cora	2708	5429	1433	7
	Citeseer	3312	4732	3708	6

We implemented the ACGAT based on the PyTorch framework. All the three datasets were split into training, validation, and test subsets with a ratio of 8:1:1. In all experiments, two layers of the ACGAT were used, and Adam was used as the optimizer. The learning rate was 0.005. For input features and normalized attention coefficients, we used a dropout rate of 0.6 and L2 regularization with a full attenuation of 0.0005.

5.2. Experimental Analysis

We dealt with the three datasets individually. When the authors in the scholar cooperation network of the the SIG had the same name, we adopted the method of "author name + organization" to determine unique authors. The cooperation intensity between authors was the feature of the association commonality between nodes. In the citation network datasets, Cora and Citeseer, we calculated the shortest path between nodes as the feature of the association commonality between nodes and constructed an incidence matrix of the citation networks for node classification. The three networks constructed with this method are shown in Figure 6, in which the isolated nodes in the datasets are removed from the Citeseer network diagram. Different sizes of nodes in the network graph indicate the influence of academic resources on the network graph. Large nodes have great influence on adjacent nodes and obvious aggregation effects.

We compared the proposed method with five existing benchmark methods—DeepWalk [11], LINE (2nd) [12], structural deep network embedding (SDNE) [31], a graph convolutional network (GCN) [19], and a graph attention network (GAT) [20]. We also compared it with versions of the proposed model that only add the association commonality feature (A-GAT) or only add the association influence factor (C-GAT). Due to space limitations, we show only visualized classification results of the traditional methods (Figures 7–9). We used classification accuracy as the experimental index, which was obtained from Equation (11) [32].

$$\text{Accuracy} = \frac{TP + TN}{TP + FP + TN + FN}, \tag{11}$$

where TP (true positives) is the number of positive cases that are correctly classified. FP (false positives) is the number of false positive cases. FN (false negatives) is the number of false negatives. TN (true negatives) is the number of cases that are correctly classified as negative.

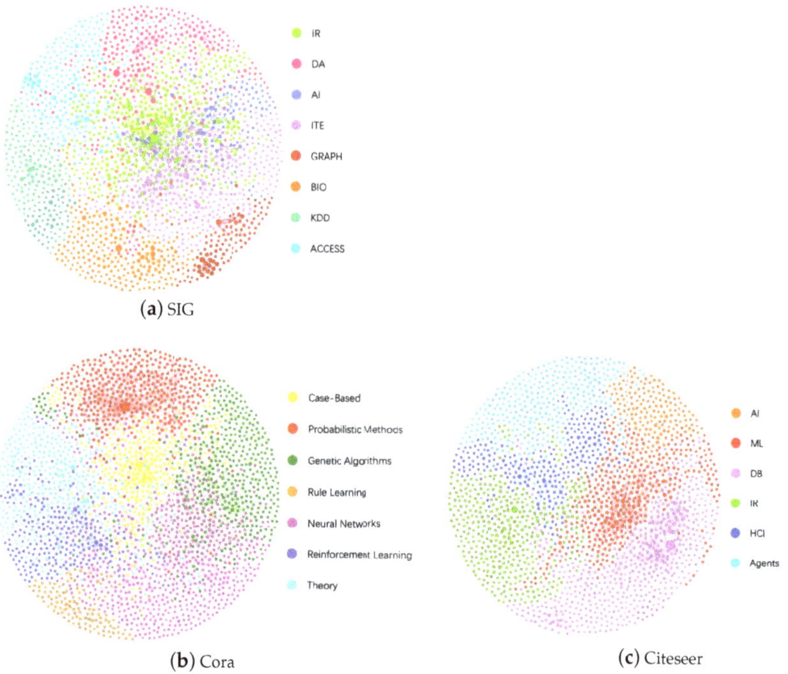

(a) SIG

(b) Cora

(c) Citeseer

Figure 6. The networks constructed for the three datasets. (**a**) SIG scholar collaboration network. (**b**) Cora citation network. (**c**) Citeseer citation network. In the networks, different colors represent different categories, and the size of a node represents its influence on other nodes.

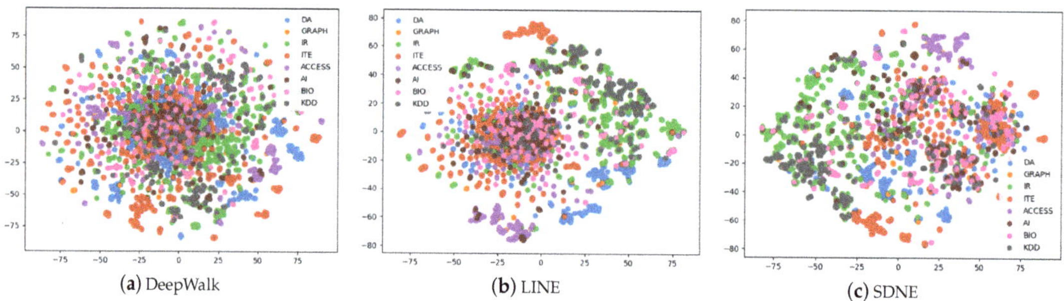

(a) DeepWalk

(b) LINE

(c) SDNE

Figure 7. A comparison of the visualization results of the three methods for the SIG dataset. (**a**) The result of DeepWalk, (**b**) the result of LINE, and (**c**) the result of structural deep network embedding (SDNE). Differently colored nodes represent different categories. The dataset contains eight categories (Ada programming language (DA); computer graphics (GRAPH); information retrieval (IR); information technology education (ITE); accessibility and computing (ACCESS); artificial intelligence (AI); computational biology (BIO); knowledge discovery in data (KDD)).

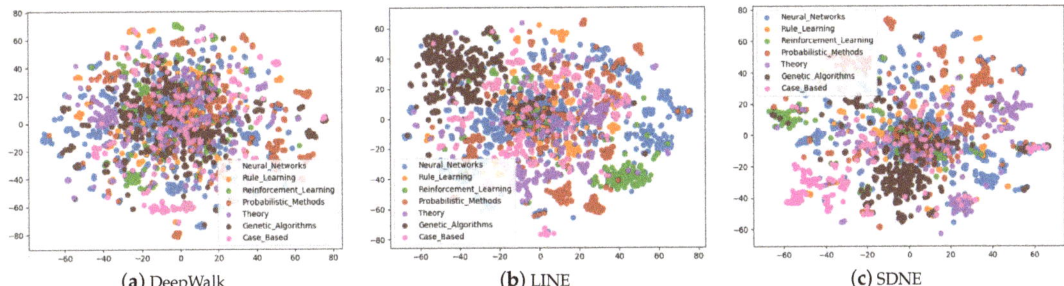

Figure 8. A comparison of the visualization results of the three methods for the Cora dataset. (**a**) The result of DeepWalk, (**b**) the result of LINE, and (**c**) the result of SDNE. Differently colored nodes represent different categories. The dataset contains seven categories (neural networks; rule learning; reinforcement learning; probability methods; theory; genetic algorithms; case-based).

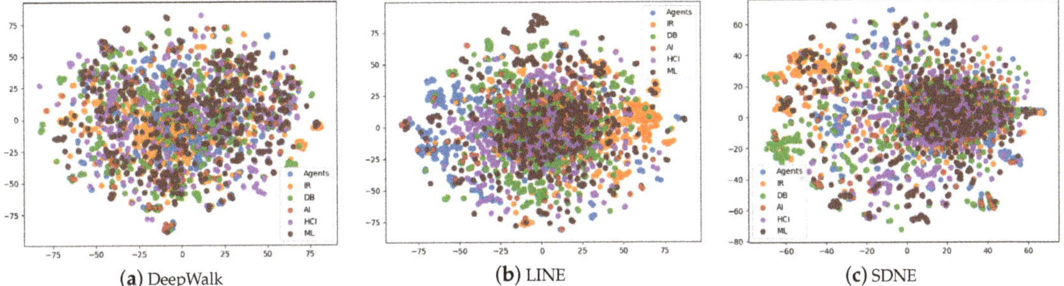

Figure 9. A comparison of the visualization results of the three methods for the Citeseer dataset. (**a**) The result of DeepWalk, (**b**) the result of LINE, and (**c**) the result of SDNE. Differently colored nodes represent different categories. The dataset contains six categories (agents; artificial intelligence (AI); database (DB); information retrieval (IR); machine language (ML); human–computer interaction (HCI)).

The classification results for scholars in the SIG are shown in Figure 10. The classification results for papers in the Cora and Citeseer citation networks are shown in Figure 11.

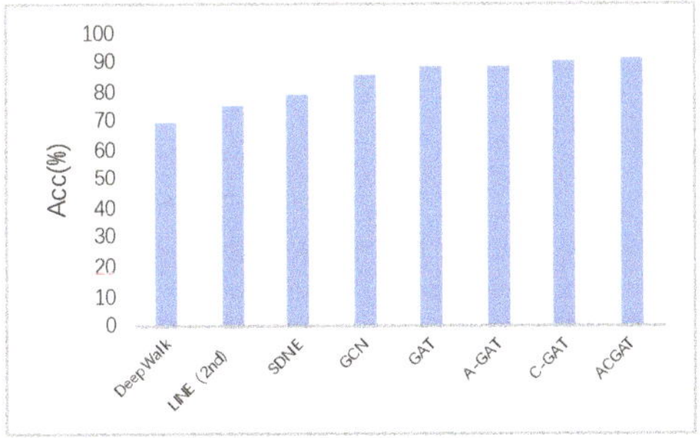

Figure 10. Classification results for SIG.

In the experiment on the scholar network dataset SIG, the use of A-GAT means that only the cooperation intensity relationships between scholars are added as the association commonality feature for the model; the use of C-GAT means that only the weights of the scholar nodes were added as the content influence feature for the model. As shown in

Figure 10, the ACGAT achieves the best classification results compared with the other seven models. It shows that in the scholar network, under the original expression of the authors' academic similarities, combining the cooperation intensity between the authors and an author's influence weight can effectively improve the division of an author's field.

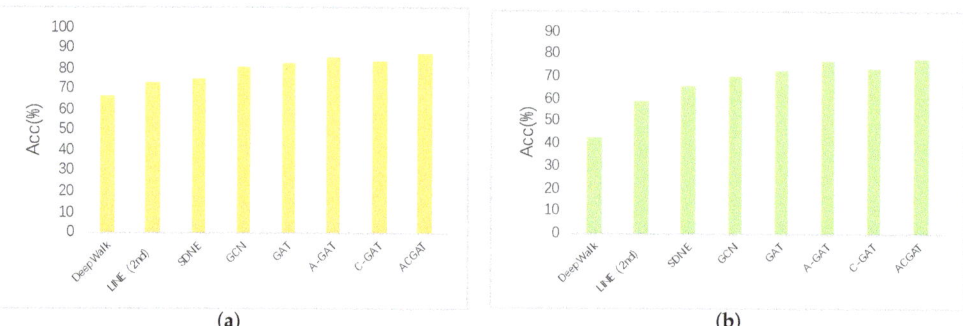

Figure 11. (**a**) Classification results for Cora. (**b**) Classification results for Citeseer.

Similarly, in the experiments on the Cora and Citeseer citation network datasets, A-GAT only adds the citation association commonality information between papers, that is, combining the shortest distance information between nodes; C-GAT only adds the weight of paper nodes as the feature of content influence. As shown in Figure 11, ACGAT also obtains the best classification result compared with other seven models. The results show that in the citation network, under the original paper feature representation, the combination of the papers' similarity and structure relevance information can effectively improve the classification results of electronic academic resources. However, after combining the commonality features and influence information on Citeseer, the classification effect is not improved much compared with the A-GAT. The reason is that the classification in the Citeseer dataset is more general than that in the Cora dataset, and there are some isolated nodes, which affects the classification effect.

In addition to the classification accuracy, we also compared the Micro-F1 [32] and Macro-F1 [33] of the models. Equations (12)–(14) [34] and explanations of the two indices are given in the following.

$$\text{Precision} = \frac{TP}{TP + FP} \tag{12}$$

$$\text{Recall} = \frac{TP}{(TP + FN)} \tag{13}$$

$$\text{F1} = 2 \times \frac{\text{Precision} \times \text{Recall}}{\text{Precision} + \text{Recall}} \tag{14}$$

- Micro-F1: We calculate this metric globally by counting the total true positives, false negatives, and false positives, and then calculate F1.
- Macro-F1: We calculate this metric for each label and find its unweighted mean. This does not take label imbalance into account.

The experimental results are shown in Table 3. In addition, we compared the accuracy curves over 300 epochs (one epoch is when all of the training samples have a forward propagation and a back propagation in the neural network) of five graph neural network models, including the model that we present in this paper. The curve comparison diagrams are shown in Figures 12–14, which prove the reliability of our model.

Table 3. Micro-F1 and Macro-F1 of various algorithms.

Dataset Metrics (%)	SIG		Cora		Citeseer	
	Micro-F1	Macro-F1	Micro-F1	Macro-F1	Micro-F1	Macro-F1
DeepWalk	60.91	53.66	57.75	54.12	41.63	35.70
LINE	65.28	56.52	62.55	61.23	54.49	49.34
SDNE	69.23	60.01	70.11	67.47	60.01	55.38
GCN	75.31	69.32	78.72	71.38	64.35	58.21
GAT	80.20	77.65	86.83	78.84	68.72	64.36
A-GAT	83.11	75.27	88.71	83.26	73.26	69.24
C-GAT	86.26	81.39	88.43	85.17	71.11	66.83
ACGAT	90.67	85.22	92.62	88.54	74.69	70.30

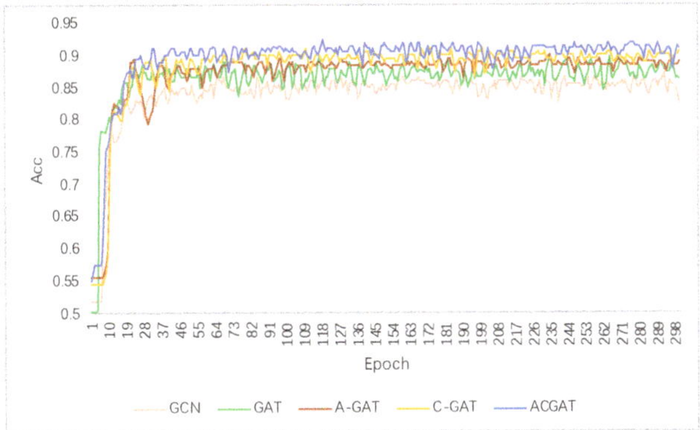

Figure 12. The comparison results of neural network models on the SIG scholar network.

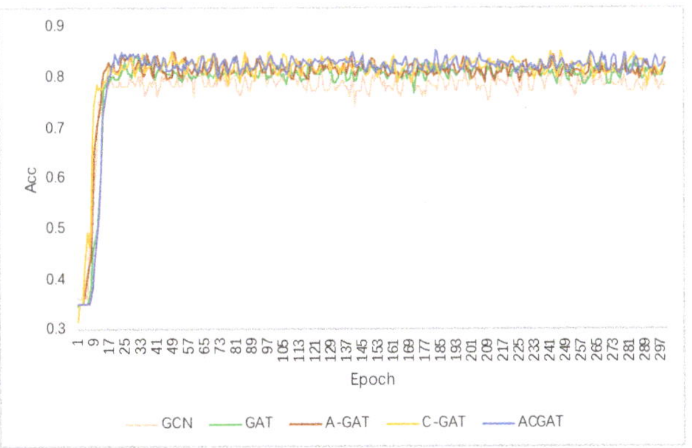

Figure 13. Comparison results of neural network models on the Cora citation network.

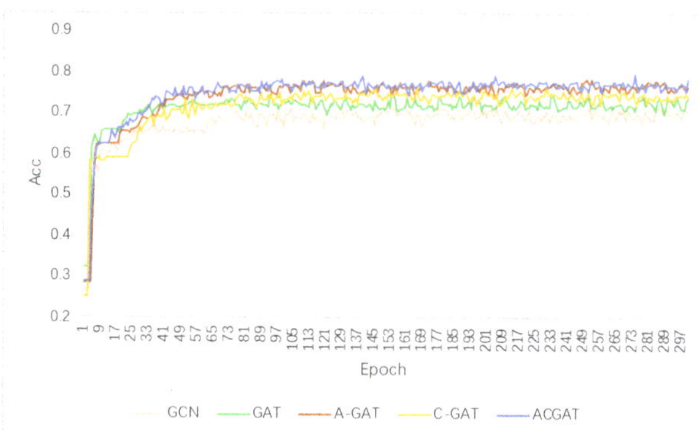

Figure 14. Comparison results of neural network models on the Citeseer citation network.

From Table 3 and Figures 7–9, we can observe that the performance of the network representation learning method DeepWalk, which is based on a random walk, and the LINE method, which is based on the assumption of domain similarity, was not good for the three academic resource datasets, and they could not effectively classify different types of nodes. This indicates that more similar nodes have the same vector representations with a certain deviation by relying on simple empirical indicators, which cannot reflect the structural characteristics around the nodes well. In contrast, SDNE, which is based on deep learning, achieved better classification results than the traditional methods. SDNE performed better in the self-built scholar cooperation network, SIG, and the Cora citation network, but the node classification effect was still unsatisfactory due to the limited modeling ability.

The GCN assigned the same weights to the domain nodes [35], and its classification effect was inferior to that of the GAT. By introducing the attention mechanism, the graph attention network calculated the weight of each node's neighbor nodes and learned to allocate different aggregation coefficients to obtain new features of nodes. The A-GAT, C-GAT, and ACGAT proposed in this paper are all based on the GAT combined with the edge information and the influence information. The ACGAT mines the resource association features and content attributes and integrates an attention mechanism to update the node features of academic resources. Figures 12–14 show that the ACGAT has better effectiveness than the existing classification methods.

6. Conclusions

The classification of academic resources has important research status and practical significance. This paper mainly studies the use of academic resources to aggregate domain information for classification. We focused on the content attributes, structure attributes, and the edge attribute information of academic resources. The proposed model combines the academic semantic relevance, academic association commonality, and association influence factors to describe the characteristics of an academic resource network in order to mine more abundant information. At the same time, the attention mechanism is used to model and learn the different coefficients to get the best proportional distribution. We conducted experiments on a self-built scholar network dataset and public citation network datasets. The experimental results show that the algorithm in this paper has an improvement of 2.5–4.7% compared with the original graph attention network, and the classification effect is better than that of other existing methods. In addition to academic resource classification tasks, the ACGAT is also suitable for dealing with other social network classification tasks that are based on graph data. In the future, we will improve the model to realize the classification of heterogeneous vertices in academic networks.

Author Contributions: Conceptualization, Y.L. and J.Y.; methodology, Y.L. and J.Y.; validation, Y.L., C.P., and J.W.; investigation, Y.L.; resources, Y.L. and J.Y; data curation, Y.L.; writing—original draft preparation, Y.L.; writing—review and editing, Y.L and J.Y.; visualization, Y.L. All authors have read and agreed to the published version of the manuscript.

Funding: This research received no external funding.

Data Availability Statement: Prithviraj Sen, Galileo Namata, Mustafa Bilgic, Lise Getoor, Brian Galligher, and Tina Eliassi-Rad. Collective classification in network data. AI magazine, 29(3):93, 2008. The data for the self-built dataset (SIG) came from https://dl.acm.org/sigs (accessed on 4 March 2021).

Conflicts of Interest: The authors declare no conflict of interest.

References

1. Lin, S.; Zheng, D. Big Data to Lead a New Era for "Internet+": Current Status and Prospect. In *Proceedings of the Fourth International Forum on Decision Sciences*; Li, X., Xu, X., Eds.; Springer: Singapore, 2017; pp. 245–252.
2. Fidalgo-Blanco, A.; Sánchez-Canales, M.; Sein-Echaluce, M.L.; García-Peñalvo, F.J. Ontological Search for Academic Resources. In Proceedings of the Sixth International Conference on Technological Ecosystems for Enhancing Multiculturality, Salamanca, Spain, 24–26 October 2018.
3. Guo, G. Decision support system for manuscript submissions to academic journals: An example of submitting an enterprise resource planning manuscript. In Proceedings of the 2017 International Conference on Machine Learning and Cybernetics (ICMLC), Ningbo, China, 9–12 July 2017.
4. Correia, F.F.; Aguiar, A. Patterns of Information Classification. In Proceedings of the 18th Conference on Pattern Languages of Programs, Portland, OR, USA, 21–23October 2011.
5. Gong, L.; Cheng, Q. Exploiting Edge Features for Graph Neural Networks. In Proceedings of the IEEE/CVF Conference on Computer Vision and Pattern Recognition (CVPR), Long Beach, CA, USA, 15–21 June 2019.
6. Sina, S.; Rosenfeld, A.; Kraus, S. Solving the Missing Node Problem Using Structure and Attribute Information. In Proceedings of the 2013 IEEE/ACM International Conference on Advances in Social Networks Analysis and Mining, Niagara Falls, ON, Canada, 25–28 August 2013.
7. Fei, H.; Huan, J. Boosting with Structure Information in the Functional Space: An Application to Graph Classification. In Proceedings of the 16th ACM SIGKDD International Conference on Knowledge Discovery and Data Mining, Washington, DC, USA, 24–28 July 2010.
8. Chen, S.; Huang, S.; Yuan, D.; Zhao, X. A Survey of Algorithms and Applications Related with Graph Embedding. In Proceedings of the 2020 International Conference on Cyberspace Innovation of Advanced Technologies, Guangzhou, China, 4–6 December 2020.
9. Ahmed, A.; Shervashidze, N.; Narayanamurthy, S.; Josifovski, V.; Smola, A.J. Distributed Large-Scale Natural Graph Factorization. In *Proceedings of the 22nd International Conference on World Wide Web*; Association for Computing Machinery: New York, NY, USA, 2013; pp. 37–48. [CrossRef]
10. Cao, S.; Lu, W.; Xu, Q. GraRep. In Proceedings of the 24th ACM International on Conference on Information and Knowledge Management-CIKM, Melbourne, Australia, 19–23 October 2015.
11. Perozzi, B.; Al-Rfou, R.; Skiena, S. DeepWalk: Online Learning of Social Representations. In Proceedings of the 20th ACM SIGKDD International Conference on Knowledge Discovery and Data Mining, New York, NY, USA, 24–27 August 2014.
12. Tang, J.; Qu, M.; Wang, M.; Zhang, M.; Yan, J.; Mei, Q. LINE: Large-scale Information Network Embedding. *Line Large-Scale Inf. Netw. Embed.* **2015**. [CrossRef]
13. Grover, A.; Leskovec, J. node2vec: Scalable Feature Learning for Networks. In Proceedings of the 22nd ACM SIGKDD International Conference on Knowledge Discovery and Data Mining, San Francisco, CA, USA, 13–17 August 2016.
14. Zheng, D.; Wang, M.; Gan, Q.; Zhang, Z.; Karypis, G. Learning Graph Neural Networks with Deep Graph Library. In Proceedings of the Companion Proceedings of the Web Conference 2020, Taipei, Taiwan, 20–24 April 2020.
15. Song, X.; Yang, H.; Zhou, C. Pedestrian Attribute Recognition with Graph Convolutional Network in Surveillance Scenarios. *Future Internet* **2019**, *11*. [CrossRef]
16. Zhang, C.; Song, D.; Huang, C.; Swami, A.; Chawla, N.V. Heterogeneous Graph Neural Network. In Proceedings of the 25th ACM SIGKDD International Conference on Knowledge Discovery & Data Mining, Anchorage, AK, USA, 4–8 August 2019.
17. Che, M.; Yao, K.; Che, C.; Cao, Z.; Kong, F. Knowledge-Graph-Based Drug Repositioning against COVID-19 by Graph Convolutional Network with Attention Mechanism. *Future Internet* **2021**, *13*, 13. [CrossRef]
18. Niepert, M.; Ahmed, M.; Kutzkov, K. Learning Convolutional Neural Networks for Graphs. In *International Conference on Machine Learning*; PMLR: Cambridge, MA, USA, 2016.
19. Kipf, T.N.; Welling, M. Semi-Supervised Classification with Graph Convolutional Networks. *arXiv* **2016**, arXiv:1609.02907.
20. Veličković, P.; Cucurull, G.; Casanova, A.; Romero, A.; Lio, P.; Bengio, Y. Graph Attention Networks. *arXiv* **2017**, arXiv:1710.10903.

21. Gilmer, J.; Schoenholz, S.; Riley, P.; Vinyals, O.; Dahl, G. Neural Message Passing for Quantum Chemistry. In *International Conference on Machine Learning*; PMLR: Cambridge, MA, USA, 2017.
22. Lin, L.; Wang, H. Graph Attention Networks over Edge Content-Based Channels. In Proceedings of the 26th ACM SIGKDD International Conference on Knowledge Discovery & Data Mining, San Diego, CA, USA, 22 August 2020.
23. Shanthamallu, U.S.; Thiagarajan, J.J.; Spanias, A. A Regularized Attention Mechanism for Graph Attention Networks. In Proceedings of the ICASSP 2020—2020 IEEE International Conference on Acoustics, Speech and Signal Processing (ICASSP), Barcelona, Spain, 4–8 May 2020.
24. Zhukovskiy, M.; Gusev, G.; Serdyukov, P. Supervised Nested PageRank. In Proceedings of the 23rd ACM International Conference on Conference on Information and Knowledge Management, Shanghai, China, 3–7 November 2014.
25. Meyer-Brötz, F.; Schiebel, E.; Brecht, L. Experimental evaluation of parameter settings in calculation of hybrid similarities: Effects of first- and second-order similarity, edge cutting, and weighting factors. *Scientometrics* **2017**, *111*, 1307–1325. [CrossRef]
26. Ortega-Arranz, H.; R. Llanos, D.; Gonzalez-Escribano, A. The shortest-path problem: Analysis and comparison of methods. *Synth. Lect. Theor. Comput. Sci.* **2014**, *1*, 1–87. [CrossRef]
27. Low, J.X.; Choo, K.W. Classification of Heart Sounds Using Softmax Regression and Convolutional Neural Network. In Proceedings of the 2018 International Conference on Communication Engineering and Technology, Singapore, 24–26 February 2018.
28. Jiang, T.; Cheng, J. Target Recognition Based on CNN with LeakyReLU and PReLU Activation Functions. In Proceedings of the 2019 International Conference on Sensing, Diagnostics, Prognostics, and Control (SDPC), Beijing, China, 15–17 August 2019.
29. Jia, X.; Li, W. Text classification model based on multi-head attention capsule neworks. *J. Tsinghua Univ. (Sci. Technol.)* **2020**, *60*, 415. [CrossRef]
30. Sen, P.; Namata, G.; Bilgic, M.; Getoor, L.; Galligher, B.; Eliassi-Rad, T. Collective Classification in Network Data. *AI Mag.* **2008**, *29*, 93. [CrossRef]
31. Wang, D.; Cui, P.; Zhu, W. Structural Deep Network Embedding. In *Proceedings of the 22nd ACM SIGKDD International Conference on Knowledge Discovery and Data Mining*; Association for Computing Machinery: New York, NY, USA, 2016; pp. 1225–1234. [CrossRef]
32. Vidyapu, S.; Vedula, V.S.; Bhattacharya, S. Quantitative Visual Attention Prediction on Webpage Images Using Multiclass SVM. In Proceedings of the 11th ACM Symposium on Eye Tracking Research & Applications, Denver, CO, USA, 25–28 June 2019.
33. Lin, Z.; Lyu, S.; Cao, H.; Xu, F.; Wei, Y.; Samet, H.; Li, Y. HealthWalks: Sensing Fine-Grained Individual Health Condition via Mobility Data. *Proc. ACM Interactive Mobile Wearable Ubiquitous Technol.* **2020**, *4*, 1–26. [CrossRef]
34. Shim, H.; Luca, S.; Lowet, D.; Vanrumste, B. Data Augmentation and Semi-Supervised Learning for Deep Neural Networks-Based Text Classifier. In Proceedings of the 35th Annual ACM Symposium on Applied Computing, Brno, Czech Republic, 30 March–3 April 2020.
35. Chen, Y.; Hu, S.; Zou, L. An In-depth Analysis of Graph Neural Networks for Semi-supervised Learning. In *Semantic Technology*; Wang, X., Lisi, F.A., Xiao, G., Botoeva, E., Eds.; Springer: Singapore, 2020; pp. 65–77.

 *future internet*

Article

Pat-in-the-Loop: Declarative Knowledge for Controlling Neural Networks

Dario Onorati [1], Pierfrancesco Tommasino [1], Leonardo Ranaldi [2], Francesca Fallucchi [2,*] and Fabio Massimo Zanzotto [1,*]

1 Department of Enterprise Engineering, University of Rome Tor Vergata, 00133 Roma, Italy; darionorati@gmail.com (D.O.); tommasinofrancesco93@gmail.com (P.T.)

2 Department of Innovation and Information Engineering, Guglielmo Marconi University, 00193 Roma, Italy; l.ranaldi@unimarconi.it

* Correspondence: f.fallucchi@unimarconi.it (F.F.); fabio.massimo.zanzotto@uniroma2.it (F.M.Z.)

Received: 22 October 2020; Accepted: 28 November 2020; Published: 2 Decemebr 2020

Abstract: The dazzling success of neural networks over natural language processing systems is imposing an urgent need to control their behavior with simpler, more direct declarative rules. In this paper, we propose Pat-in-the-Loop as a model to control a specific class of syntax-oriented neural networks by adding declarative rules. In Pat-in-the-Loop, *distributed tree encoders* allow to exploit parse trees in neural networks, *heat parse trees* visualize activation of parse trees, and parse subtrees are used as declarative rules in the neural network. Hence, Pat-in-the-Loop is a model to include human control in specific natural language processing (NLP)-neural network (NN) systems that exploit syntactic information, which we will generically call Pat. A pilot study on question classification showed that declarative rules representing human knowledge, injected by Pat, can be effectively used in these neural networks to ensure correctness, relevance, and cost-effective.

Keywords: NLP; machine learning; deep learning; AI; human-in-the-loop

---

1. Introduction

Neural networks are obtaining dazzling successes in natural language processing (NLP). General neural networks learned on terabytes of data are replacing decades of scientific investigations by showing unprecedented performances in a variety of NLP tasks [1]. Hence, systems based on NLP and on neural networks (NLP-NN) are everywhere.

As a consequence of their success, public opinion is extremely fast in spotting possibly catastrophic, unwanted behavior on deployed NLP-NN systems (see, for example, [2,3]). As many learned systems [4,5], NLP-NN systems are also exposed to biased decisions or biased production of utterances. This problem is becoming so important that extensive analyses are performed, for example, for the tricky class of systems for sentiment analysis [6].

To promptly recover from catastrophic failures, NLP-NN systems should be endowed with the possibility of modifying their behavior by using declarative languages. Deductive teaching is an extremely difficult task even in the human learning process [7,8]. Active learning techniques [9,10] can require too many examples and may focus the attention of NLP-NN systems on irrelevant peculiarities of datasets [11]. Usually we do not have the time or budget for human input on every data point, and so need strategies for deciding which data points are the most important for human review. Due to the high costs to obtain human-generated activity data using solutions for which a very limited number of examples with supervised information such as Few-Shot Learning or One-shot learning [12,13] could be used. But the core issue of these techniques is the unreliable empirical risk minimizer that makes them hard to learn. Understanding the core issue helps categorize different works into data, model and algorithm according to how they solve the core issue using prior knowledge: data augments the supervised experience, model constrains the hypothesis space to be smaller, and algorithm alters the search strategy for the best hypothesis in the given hypothesis space [14]. But this is exactly what we want to fight in favour of approaches that understanding neural networks and trying to control their behavior besides using training examples.

Looking into NLP-NN systems beyond the dazzling light is becoming an active area [15,16], since traditional neural network visualization tools are obscure when applied to NLP-NN systems. Heatmaps are powerful tools for visualizing neural networks applied to image interpretation [17]. In fact, heatmaps can visualize how neural network layers treat specific subparts of images. Yet, when applied to NLP-NN systems [18] they are extremely difficult to interpret. For this reason, human involvement with the right interfaces could expedite the efficient labeling of tricky or novel data that a machine can't process, reducing the potential for data-related errors.

In this paper, we propose *Pat-in-the-Loop* as a model to include human control in specific NLP-NN systems that exploit syntactic information. The key contributions are: (1) *distributed tree encoders* that directly exploit parse trees in neural networks; (2) *heat parse trees* that visualize which parts of parse trees are responsible for the activation of specific neurons (see Figure 1); and (3) a declarative language for controlling the behavior of neural networks.

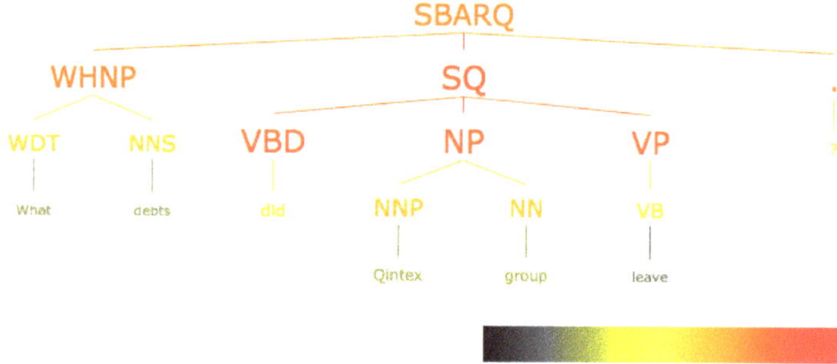

Figure 1. A heat parse tree.

Distributed tree encoders allow to produce heat parse trees and developers can explore activation of parse trees for specific decisions to derive rules for correcting system behavior.

In the following work, we performed a pilot study on question classification where *Pat-in-the-Loop* showed that human knowledge can be effectively used to control the behavior of a syntactic NLP-NN system.

In the next section (Section 2) we report the related works about the visualization of neural networks models. Next follow a description of Pat-in-the-Loop works (Section 3) and finally (Section 4), we show the improvements achieved by the proposed model.

2. Related Work

In recent years with the advent of neural networks, many methods to visualize neural networks have been developed. The most common methods to display neural networks is using a *node-link graph* where nodes depict computational units and *edge weights* indicate an input-output connection between these nodes. Generally, for ease of understanding and to encourage the user, the magnitude of a parameter or activation is displayed using different colors and sizes for the *edge weights*.

For example, *ActiVis* [19] offers a view of neuron activations and can be used to view interactive model interpretations of large heterogeneous data formats such as images and text.

ActiVis can closely integrate multiple coordinated views, such as a model architecture calculation graph and a neuron activation view for model discovery and comparison, users can explore complex models of deep neural networks at both instance and subset level. Although it is a progressive system, *ActiVis* does not support recurrent architectures, a common type of architecture in natural language tasks.

For this extent, Ming et al. [20] and Strobelt et al. [21] proposed respectively dedicated visualizers for *recurrent neural networks (RNNviz)* and *long short-term memory networks (LSTMviz)* that are able to inspect the dynamic of the hidden state. The ultimate purpose is to show the functions of hidden state units and explain them using their expected response to input texts, i.e., words. This allows users to gain a more complete understanding and greater confidence in the hidden RNN and LSTM mechanism through various visual techniques.

Recently, with the advent of transformer models [22], a lot of work has been done in order to interpret activations of attention heads [23–25]. In this new world of multi-layered, multi-headed attention, mechanisms of the Transformer model can be difficult to decipher. To make the model more accessible, many researchers have begun to think about an open-source tool that visualizes attention at multiple scales, each of which provides a unique perspective on the attention mechanism. All these Transformer visualizers allow to view the magnitude of softmax attention heads correlated with input tokens to interpret model's decisions. By way of example, we selected *BERTviz* [23] as the representative for this category of transformer visualizers.

Embedding Projector [26] is an interactive tool for visualizing and interpreting *embeddings*. This tool uses different dimensionality reduction techniques to map high-dimensional embedding vectors into low-dimensional output vectors that are easier to visualize. It can be used to analyze the geometry of words and explore the *embedding space*, although it cannot be used directly to explain a neural network model.

The following table (Table 1) shows a sample of the most common types of visualization tools for neural networks in the context of natural language processing.

Table 1. Summary of representative visualization tools for natural language processing (NLP)-neural network (NN) systems. * our work.

Features	*	*RNNvis*	*Emb. Proj.*	*LSTMVis*	*ActiVis*	*BERTviz*
Interpretability & Explainability	x	x		x	x	x
Debbuging & Improvement Models	x			x	x	
Developer-friendly	x	x	x	x	x	x
User-friendly			x	x	x	x
Algorithm Attribution & Features Visualization	x		x			x
During Training						
After Training	x	x	x	x	x	x
NLP-NN system	x	x	x	x	x	x

From Table 1, we can observe the basic characteristics offered by the above mentioned works. The features that everyone shares are: the target audience, i.e., *Developer-Friendly*, the time of training when we can avail ourselves of these systems, i.e., *After Training* and finally the purpose of the systems themselves, i.e., improve the elements *Interpretability & Explainability*. The distinguishing features offered by our system are: the display and easy choice of the underlying model to use, i.e., *Algorithm Attribution & Features Visualization* and the ability to manipulate the model itself to improve it in a very simple way.

In addition to this visualizer, we propose *Pat-in-the-Loop* as a model to include human control in specific NLP-NN systems that exploit syntactic information. Our system allows to display *heat parse trees* that are a handy way to represent syntactic node contributions in a neural network directly into syntactic trees and a declarative language for controlling the behavior of neural networks. The following section describes in detail how it works.

3. The Model

In Pat-in-the-Loop (see Figure 2), a generic developer, which we call Pat, may inspect the reasons why her/his neural network takes some decisions. In fact, Pat's neural network model is based on *distributed tree encoders* $\mathbf{W}_{dt}$ to directly exploit parse trees in neural networks (Section 3.2). Pat can visualize why some decisions are taken from the network according to parse trees of examples x by using *"heat parse trees"* (Sections 3.1 and 3.3). Hence, Pat can control the behavior of neural networks with declarative rules represented as subtrees by encoding these rules in $\mathbf{W}_H$ (Section 3.4).

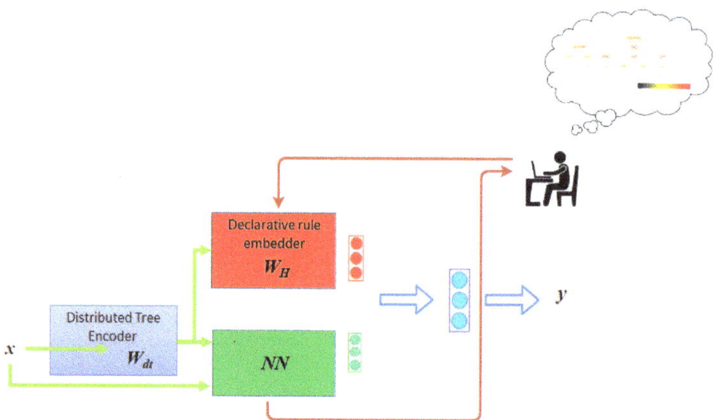

Figure 2. *Pat-in-the-Loop*: the overall system.

In other words, the key idea we propose in Pat-in-the-Loop model is using *"heat parse trees"* to analyze which parts of parse trees are responsible for the activation of specific neurons (Section 3.3); and, then, controlling the behavior of neural networks with declarative rules derived from the analysis of these heat parse trees (Section 3.4). This is a loop (see the red arrow in Figure 2) where Pat analyzes the output of the Neural Network (NN). The red block, which is the Declarative rule embedder, is a special module that allows Pat to encode declarative rules. These rules, which are embedded in special vectors (see in Section 3.4) will affect the decision of the neural network by modifying its behavior during training.

Before starting the description of the core components of the Pat-in-the-Loop model, Section 3.1 introduces some preliminary notation and the notion of heat parse trees. Below is part relating to the foundations of the proposed system Section 3.2. Then, we close with a section about the visualization (Section 3.3) and the additional layer (Section 3.4).

3.1. Preliminary Notation

Parse trees and *heat parse trees* are core representations in our model. This section introduces the notation to describe these two representations.

Parse trees $\mathcal{T}$ and parse subtrees τ are recursively represented as trees $t = (r, [t_1, \ldots, t_k])$ where r is the label representing the root of the tree and $[t_1, \ldots, t_k]$ is the list of child trees t_i. Leaves t are represented as trees $t = (r, [])$ with an empty list of children or directly as $t = r$.

Heat parse trees, similarly to "heat trees" in biology [27], are heatmaps over parse trees (see Figure 1). The underlying representation is an *active tree* $\bar{t}$, that is, a tree where an activation value

$v_r \in \mathbb{R}$ is associated to each node: $\bar{t} = (r, v_r, [\bar{t}_1, \ldots, \bar{t}_k])$. Heat parse trees are then the graphical visualization of active trees $\bar{t}$ where colors and sizes of nodes r depend on their activation values v_r.

3.2. Distributed Tree Encoders for Exploiting Parse Trees in Neural Networks

Distributed tree encoders are the encoders used in Pat-in-the-Loop to directly exploit parse trees in neural networks. These encoders, stemming from tree kernels [28] and distributed tree kernels [29], give the possibility to represent parse trees in vector spaces $\mathbb{R}^d$ that embed huge spaces of subtrees $\mathbb{R}^n$.

Tree kernels [28] have offered an important opportunity to fully exploit parse trees in learning with kernel machines [30,31]. Tree kernels are functions implicitly computing the similarity among parse trees $\mathcal{T}$ mapped in vectors $\boldsymbol{x}^{\mathcal{T}} \in \mathbb{R}^n$ where dimensions are subtrees τ. For example, the 52629-th dimension of $\boldsymbol{x}^{\mathcal{T}} \in \mathbb{R}^n$ can represent the subtree $\tau^{(52629)}$ =*(SQ,[(VBD,[did]),NP,VP])* (see Table 2). Vectors $\boldsymbol{x}^{\mathcal{T}}$ for parse trees T generally have:

$$x_i^{\mathcal{T}} = \begin{cases} \lambda^{\frac{|\tau^{(i)}|}{2}} & \text{if } \tau^{(i)} \in S(T) \\ 0 & \text{if } \tau^{(i)} \notin S(T) \end{cases}$$

where $S(\mathcal{T})$ is the set of valid subtrees of $\mathcal{T}$, $0 < \lambda < 1$ is a decay factor penalizing large subtrees, and $|\tau^{(i)}|$ is the size of the node set of $\tau^{(i)}$. Valid subtrees $\tau \in S(\mathcal{T})$ in [28] are connected subtrees of $\mathcal{T}$ of at least two nodes and, if τ contains a node c, it should contains all the siblings of the node c in $\mathcal{T}$. For example, $x_{52629}^{\mathcal{T}_e} = \lambda^{\frac{5}{2}}$ for the parse tree in Figure 1 since $\tau^{(52629)}$ is a valid subtree of $\mathcal{T}_e$. The power of these tree kernels is that parse trees are are never explicitly represented as vectors $\boldsymbol{x}^{\mathcal{T}}$ but the tree kernel functions implicitly compute their dot product.

Table 2. Sample of a subtree space with activation of the target layer $\boldsymbol{o}$.

Dim in $\mathbb{R}^n$	*Represented Subtree*	**Target Output** o ...	o_{27}	...
...	...	...	...	...
$\tau^{(52628)}$	*(VP,[VBP,([NP,[(DT,[a])]),NN)])*	...	−0.001	...
$\tau^{(52629)}$	*(SQ,[(VBD,[did]),NP,VP])*	...	0.11	...
$\tau^{(52630)}$	*(NP,[DT,(NN,[lottery])])*	...	0.0002	...
$\tau^{(52631)}$	*(WHNP,[(WDT,[What]),NNS])*	...	0.07	...
...	...	...	...	...

Distributed tree kernels [29] may transfer the opportunity given by tree kernels [28] within neural networks since distributed tree kernels implicitly embed vectors $\boldsymbol{x}^{\mathcal{T}} \in \mathbb{R}^n$ into a reduced space $\mathbb{R}^d$ in the context of support vector machines. Distributed tree kernels build on Johnson–Lindenstrauss Transformation [32] and holographic reduced representations (HRR) [33].

Building on distributed tree kernels, we propose *distributed tree encoders* that may be seen as linear transformations $\boldsymbol{W}_{dt} \in \mathbb{R}^{d \times n}$ (similarly to Johnson–Lindenstrauss Transformation [32]). These linear transformations embed vectors $\boldsymbol{x}^{\mathcal{T}} \in \mathbb{R}^n$ in the space of tree kernels in smaller vectors $\boldsymbol{y}^{\mathcal{T}} \in \mathbb{R}^d$:

$$\boldsymbol{y}^{\mathcal{T}} = \boldsymbol{W}_{dt} \boldsymbol{x}^{\mathcal{T}}$$

Columns $\boldsymbol{w}_i$ of $\boldsymbol{W}_{dt}$ encode subtree $\tau^{(i)}$ and are computed with an encoding function $\boldsymbol{w}_i = E(\tau^{(i)})$ as follows:

$$E(\tau^{(i)}) = \begin{cases} \boldsymbol{r} & \text{if } \tau^{(i)} = (r, []) \\ \boldsymbol{r} \otimes E(\tau_1^{(i)}) \otimes \ldots \otimes E(\tau_k^{(i)}) & \\ & \text{if } \tau^{(i)} = (r, [\tau_1^{(i)}, \ldots, \tau_k^{(i)}]) \end{cases} \quad (1)$$

where the operation $\boldsymbol{u} \otimes \boldsymbol{v}$ is the shuffled circular convolution, that is, a circular convolution $\star$ (as for HRR [33]) with a permutation matrix Φ: $\boldsymbol{u} \otimes \boldsymbol{v} = \boldsymbol{u} * \Phi \boldsymbol{v}$; and, $\boldsymbol{r} \sim \mathcal{N}(0, \frac{1}{\sqrt{d}}\mathbb{I})$ is drawn from a multivariate gaussian distribution.

As for tree kernels also for distributed tree encoders, linear transformations $\boldsymbol{W}_{dt}$ and vectors $\boldsymbol{x}^{\mathcal{T}} \in \mathbb{R}^n$ are never explicitly produced and encoders are implemented as recursive functions [29].

3.3. Visualizing Activation of Parse Trees

Distributed tree encoders give the possibility of using *heat parse trees* to visualize the activation of parse trees in final decisions or intermediate neuron outputs.

To compute of *active trees* $\bar{t}$ useful to produce *heat parse trees*, a neural network should be sliced at the desired layer. Let NN be the sliced neural network, $\boldsymbol{x} = \boldsymbol{x}^{\mathcal{T}}, \boldsymbol{x}^r$ and $\boldsymbol{o}$ its output:

$$\boldsymbol{o} = \mathrm{NN}(\boldsymbol{W}_{dt}\boldsymbol{x}^{\mathcal{T}}, \boldsymbol{x}^r)$$

where, given an example x, $\boldsymbol{x}^{\mathcal{T}}$ is the vector representing the tree $\mathcal{T}$ in the space of subtrees related to the example x, $\boldsymbol{W}_{dt}$ is the distributed tree encoder, and $\boldsymbol{x}^r$ is the rest of the features associated to x.

Using parse trees $\mathcal{T}$ in neural networks is straightforward with distributed trees. In fact, distributed trees $\boldsymbol{y}^{\mathcal{T}} = \boldsymbol{W}_{dt}\boldsymbol{x}^{\mathcal{T}}$ for parse trees $\mathcal{T}$ may be directly used in neural networks as these distributed trees are vectors.

Our heat parse trees show the overlap of activation of subtrees in $S(\mathcal{T})$ of specific trees $\mathcal{T}$ related to a specific example x in a specific net. This shows how subtrees in $S(\mathcal{T})$ contribute to the final activation o_i, that is, a dimension of $\boldsymbol{o}$. We believe this is more convenient than representing an extremely large heatmap for the list of subtrees in $S(\mathcal{T})$ and their related value o_i (see Table 2).

The computation of active trees $\bar{t}$ for displaying heat parse trees is the following. The activation weight v_r of each node r represents how much the node is responsible for the activation of the overall syntactic tree for the output of the given neuron o_i. Then, the activation value v_r is computed as follows:

$$v_r = \sum_{\tau \in S(T) \text{ and } r \in \tau} \mathrm{NN}(\boldsymbol{W}_{dt}\lambda^{\frac{|\tau|}{2}}\boldsymbol{\tau}, \boldsymbol{x}_r)$$

where $\boldsymbol{\tau}$ is the one-hot vector in the subtree space that indicates the subtree τ and $r \in \tau$ detects in r is node in τ.

With the above computation of $\bar{t}$, active subtrees τ for the output o_i of a specific neuron are overlapped in single heat parse trees.

The activation value can be calculated in other ways, for example using Layer-wise Relevance Propagation (LRP) [34]. They compute activation value v_r in *active tree* $\bar{t}$ by using LRP, that is a framework to explain the decisions of a generic neural network using local redistribution rules and is able to explain which input features contributed most to the final classification. This method unfortunately does not allow you to split the network at the desired layer, so it has not been taken into account.

3.4. Human-in-the-Loop Layer

Pat now has an important possibility of understanding why decisions are taken by a specific network and, hence, s/he can define specific rules to control the behavior of the neural network. By looking at the activation of specific neurons for specific examples, Pat can understand why the decision has been made. For example, the heat parse tree in Figure 1 suggests that the subtree *(SQ,[VBD,NP,VP])* is the more active in generating the decision if this is taken for the output of a neuron that represents a final class.

If Pat aims to correct the behavior of the system for a given output, s/he selects the specific instances, derives some declarative rules and embeds these rules into the network to control its behavior. More specifically, Pat selects a subtree τ and insert $E(\tau)$ as a row in matrix $\mathbf{W}_H$ that embeds *declarative rules* (see Figure 2). This specific rule will affect the decisions made by the network on the example under review and all similar examples when the neural network is re-trained after rule injection in $\mathbf{W}_H$.

The actual procedure to build up the matrix $\mathbf{W}_H$ is the following. Let us say that Pat aims to capture k different groups of characteristics s/he assumes to be important to control the behavior of the neural network. For each group i, s/he selects a set S_i of subtrees $\tau^{(i)}$ corresponding to the i-th characteristic. The matrix $\mathbf{W}_H$ is then the following:

$$\mathbf{W}_H = \begin{pmatrix} - & w_1 & - \\ - & w_2 & - \\ & \dots & \\ - & w_k & - \end{pmatrix}$$

where $w_i = \sum_{\tau^{(i)} \in S_i} E(\tau^{(i)})$ and $E(\tau^{(i)})$ is specified in Equation (1).

Hence, the matrix $\mathbf{W}_H$ is the editable component of the overall system and the procedure to build-up the matrix $\mathbf{W}_H$ offers an actionable procedure for allowing external agents, that is, Pats, to interact with this neural network-based system. The matrix $\mathbf{W}_H$ can definitely allow external agents to manipulate the behavior of the neural network by encoding rules capturing characteristics they consider relevant for a specific task.

4. Pilot Experiment

We experimented with Pat-in-the-Loop by using a question classification dataset [35]. This data helps to classify the given Questions into respective categories based on what type of answer it expects such as a numerical answer or a text description or a place or human name, etc. The dataset is extremely well studied and performances systems can achieve are very high also if the dataset is extremely small. Hence, the dataset offer a very intriguing possibility to run a complex experiment where a human in the loop can make the difference in calibrating the overall system.

4.1. Experimental Set-Up

We experimented with the Question Classification dataset [35], which contains 5242 training questions and 500 testing questions. We focused on the *coarse grain* classification problem with 6 target classes: Abbreviation (ABBR), Description (DESC), Entity (ENTY), Human (HUM), Location (LOC), and Numeric (NUM).

The Pat-in-the-Loop (see Figure 2) used in the experiments has the following configuration. Distributed trees $\boldsymbol{W}_{dt}\boldsymbol{x}^{\mathcal{T}}$ are encoded in a space $\mathbb{R}^d$ with $d = 4000$. The decaying factor of tree kernels is $\lambda = 0.6$. The module $\text{NN}(\boldsymbol{W}_{dt}\boldsymbol{x}^{\mathcal{T}}, \boldsymbol{x}^r)$ is a multi-layer perceptron that combines two multi-layer perceptrons: $Synt(\boldsymbol{W}_{dt}\boldsymbol{x}^{\mathcal{T}})$ and $Sem(\boldsymbol{x}^r)$. *Synt* exploit syntactic information and its output is 1800. *Sem* exploits a Bag-of-Word model of the input with word embedding input of 300 from fastText [36] and output of 180. *Synt* and *Sem* are concatenated and feed a multi-layer perceptron with two layers: 100 and 6. Finally, $\boldsymbol{W_H}$ has an input dimension of $d = 4000$ and an output dimension of 6 where 6 is the number of output categories required in the question classification dataset [35]. In this case, we have opted for $\boldsymbol{W_H}$, which encodes 6 different characteristics where each characteristic is linked to an output class. Then, the output of $\boldsymbol{W_H}$ and the output of $\text{NN}(\boldsymbol{W}_{dt}\boldsymbol{x}^{\mathcal{T}}, \boldsymbol{x}^r)$ are concatenated in a single vector that feeds a final linear layer. We used a ReLU activation function among layers. The last activation function is a softmax. The optimizer is Adam [37]. All experiments were run for 20 epochs in Keras [38]. Finally, we used the CoreNLP constituent-based parser [39] for parsing questions.

We performed a 3-fold cross validation with the training set to accumulate misclassified examples for the human learning loop. Pat inspected these examples by using heat parse tree and encoded the declarative rules in $\boldsymbol{W_H}$ (Table 3). The encoded declarative rules in $\boldsymbol{W_H}$ are encoded from this example (Figure 1) and then injected as rows in matrix $\boldsymbol{W_H}$ as described in Section 3.4

We compared three systems: *BoW* that contains only the word embedding used as a bag-of-word; *PureNN* that is the system without human knowledge; and *HumNN* that is the full system with Pat's declarative knowledge.

Table 3. Pat-in-the-Loop's f-measure

	f-measure	
	micro avg	*macro avg*
BoW	0.84	0.84
PureNN	0.93	0.91
HumNN	0.93	0.92

4.2. Results and Discussion

Results of our pilot experiment show important facts that we will examine in the following, focusing also on the limitations of this analysis.

Distributed tree encoders positively introduce syntactic information in neural networks: 0.84 to 0.93 of improvement in f-measure from *BoW* to *PureNN* (Table 3). This confirms a general trend observed in a similar experiment carried out in other classification tasks observed in [40].

The analysis of the errors in the training set produced very reasonable rules for two specific classes: Abbreviation (ABBR) and Numerical (NUM) (Table 4). For what concerns the abbreviation class, Pat selected very reasonable rules such as a question asks for the explanation of abbreviation if it contains parse subtrees representing the verbal phrases *"stand for"*, *"mean"* or the noun phrases contaning the adjective *"full"* or the noun *"abbreviation"*. For what concerns the NUM class, rules are fairly more specific or definitely more general. Important indicators that a question is asking for a numerical answer are, respectively, that the question contains WH-noun-phrases *"What debts"* or contains noun phrases which are a sequence of two proper nouns, a possessive ending, and another noun, that is, *(NP (NP (NNP)(NNP)(POS))(NN))*. This latter is a very general rule. These rules are then used to build up the matrix $\mathbf{W_H}$ used in the model with human knowledge (*HumNN*).

Table 4. Rules manually extracted for the question classification dataset.

Class	**Rule**
ABBR	*(NP (NP (DT) (JJ full) (NN)) (PP (IN)))*
ABBR	*(SQ (VBZ) (NP) (VP (VB stand) (PP (IN for))))*
ABBR	*(NN abbrevation)*
ABBR	*(VP (VB mean))*
NUM	*(WHNP (WDT What) (NNS debts))*
NUM	*(NP (NP (NNP)(NNP)(POS))(NN))*

Pat could change positively the behavior of the system although global results of the model with human knowledge (*HumNN*) are similar and even slightly higher than those of *PureNN*. On the general results, the effect on the results of the system are small. In fact, the micro-average is 0.93 for both models is 0.93 and macro average is 0.92 for *HumNN* with respect to 0.91 of *PureNN*. Looking more specifically on the confusion matrix (Table 5 and 6), we may observe that Pat has changed the behavior of the system where he wanted. Since Pat aimed to manipulate the behavior of the system in favor of the classes *ABBR* and *NUM*, s/he focused the attention to examples where *PlainNN* fails. Pat's rules coded in $\mathbf{W_H}$. After learning the new model *HumNN disturbed* by human declarative knowledge, results on the test set are encouraging. In fact, although the overall performance is unchanged, target classes have had positive improvement. Both *ABBR* and *NUM* have an additional positively classified example (Table 6). This tiny improvement suggests that the model can positively use declarative human knowledge. Finally, heat parse trees are informative. In fact, Pat could understand why some specific cases were misclassified and could select declarative rules to change the behavior of the system.

Table 5. PureNN's confusion matrices on Question Classification dataset (before human knowledge use).

	ABBR	*ENTY*	*DESC*	*HUM*	*LOC*	*NUM*
ABBR	6	0	3	0	0	0
ENTY	0	84	3	2	4	1
DESC	0	5	133	0	0	0
HUM	0	1	1	63	0	0
LOC	0	1	1	2	76	1
NUM	0	5	5	0	1	102

Table 6. HumNN's and confusion matrices on Question Classification dataset (after human knowledge use).

	ABBR	*ENTY*	*DESC*	*HUM*	*LOC*	*NUM*
ABBR	7	0	2	0	0	0
ENTY	0	83	5	3	2	1
DESC	0	3	135	0	0	0
HUM	0	3	0	62	0	0
LOC	0	4	1	1	74	1
NUM	0	3	4	1	2	103

Being a pilot study, the experiment has some intrinsic limitations. Clearly, the first limitation is the fact that the model has been experimented in a single and small dataset. However, this first pilot experiment is confirming our hypothesis. The second limitation is that we have not performed an ablation test on rules in Table 4. When adding external knowledge, introducing rules and consequently manipulating NNs processes could have negative impact on the system depending on the introduced rules to the system. However, in our pilot experiment, we introduced a very small set of rules which shows that Pat can obtain a positive variation of the behavior of the overall system. This is the major objective of the present study. In fact, globally, results of the pilot experiment confirmed our hypothesis: human can positively manipulate results of the system by inducing rules from the training set.

5. Conclusions and Future Work

In the line of understanding neural networks and trying to control their behavior besides using training examples, we presented Pat-in-the-Loop. Our model exploits syntactic information in neural networks by using *distributed tree encoders*, visualizes activation of syntactic information with *heat parse trees*, and encodes *declarative knowledge* in a neural network by keeping humans in the learning loop. Pat-in-the-Loop exploits Pat to understand why decisions are taken by a specific network and, hence, Pat can define specific rules to control the behavior of the neural network and s/he can understand why the decision has been made by looking at the activation of specific neurons for specific examples. According to our pilot study, Pat can obtain the desired change of the behavior of the overall Pat-in-the-Loop. Although giving encouraging results, our pilot experiment leaves some issues unanswered: the impact of the size of the dataset on the results and the impact of the quality of the introduced rules. These open issues will shape our future research. Hence, these encouraging results on a pilot study are a first *"declarative pat"* on neural networks applied to natural language processing, which may open a wide range of possible researches also, demonstrating as the humans in the loop is an important direction to ensure correctness, relevance, and cost-effective.

Our future plans stem on our recent result. We have expanded our approach with Kernel-inspired Encoder with Recursive Mechanism for Interpretable Trees (KERMIT) [40] and its visualizer

KERMITviz. Hence, our future goal is to analyze more carefully the interaction between the syntactic and semantic sources of information on heterogeneous tasks. Setting up a clear procedure for selecting positive declarative rules by means of ablation tests on a development set. The improvement given by this analysis may open the possibility of producing better rules for controlling the neural network. Then, we may better keep Human-in-the-loop of an Artificial Intelligence system [41].

Author Contributions: Software, D.O., P.T. and L.R.; Writing—original draft, D.O., L.R. and F.M.Z.; Writing—review & editing, F.F. All authors have read and agreed to the published version of the manuscript.

Funding: This research received no external funding.

Conflicts of Interest: The authors declare no conflict of interest.

References

1. Devlin, J.; Chang, M.; Lee, K.; Toutanova, K. BERT: Pre-training of Deep Bidirectional Transformers for Language Understanding. *arXiv* **2018**, arXiv:1810.04805.
2. Thompson, A. Google's Sentiment Analyzer Thinks Being Gay Is Bad. 2017. Available online: https://motherboard.vice.com/en_us/article/j5jmj8/google-artificial-intelligence-bias (accessed on 30 November 2020).
3. Jessup, S.; Gibson, A.; Capiola, A.; Alarcon, G.; Borders, M. Investigating the Effect of Trust Manipulations on Affect over Time in Human-Human versus Human-Robot Interactions. 2020. Available online: https://www.researchgate.net/publication/339027805_Investigating_the_Effect_of_Trust_Manipulations_on_Affect_over_Time_in_Human-Human_versus_Human-Robot_Interactions (accessed on 30 November 2020). [CrossRef]
4. Courtland, R. Bias detectives: The researchers striving to make algorithms fair. *Nature* **2018**, *558*, 357–360. [CrossRef]
5. Zou, J.; Schiebinger, L. AI can be sexist and racist—It's time to make it fair. *Nature* **2018**, *559*, 324–326. [CrossRef]
6. Kiritchenko, S.; Mohammad, S. Examining Gender and Race Bias in Two Hundred Sentiment Analysis Systems. In Proceedings of the Seventh Joint Conference on Lexical and Computational Semantics, *SEM@NAACL-HLT, New Orleans, LA, USA, 5–6 June 2018.
7. Agrusti, G.; Damiani, V.; Pasquazi, D.; Carta, P. Reading mathematics at school. Inferential reasoning on the Pythagorean Theorem [Leggere la matematica a scuola. Percorsi inferenziali sul teorema di Pitagora]. *Cadmo* **2015**, *23*, 61–85. [CrossRef]
8. Pasquazi, D. Capacità sensoriali e approccio intuitivo-geometrico nella preadolescenza: Un'indagine nelle scuole. *Cadmo* **2020**, *2020*, 79–96. [CrossRef]
9. Dasgupta, S. Analysis of a greedy active learning strategy. In *Advances in Neural Information Processing Systems 17*; Saul, L.K., Weiss, Y., Bottou, L., Eds.; MIT Press: Cambridge, MA, USA, 2005; pp. 337–344.
10. Sener, O.; Savarese, S. Active Learning for Convolutional Neural Networks: A Core-Set Approach. *arXiv* **2018**, arXiv:1708.00489.
11. Allen, G. Machine Learning: The View from Statistics. In Proceedings of the AAAS Annual Meeting, Houston, TX, 15 February 2019.
12. Fink, M. Object Classification from a Single Example Utilizing Class Relevance Metrics. In *Advances in Neural Information Processing Systems 17*; Saul, L.K., Weiss, Y., Bottou, L., Eds.; MIT Press: Vancouver, CA, January 2005; pp. 449–456.
13. Fei-Fei, L.; Fergus, R.; Perona, P. One-shot learning of object categories. *IEEE Trans. Pattern Anal. Mach. Intell.* **2006**, *28*, 2006. [CrossRef]
14. Wang, Y.; Yao, Q.; Kwok, J.; Ni, L.M. Generalizing from a Few Examples: A Survey on Few-Shot Learning. *arXiv* **2020**, arXiv:1904.05046.
15. Jang, K.R.; Myaeng, S.H.; Kim, S.B. Interpretable Word Embedding Contextualization. Available online: https://www.semanticscholar.org/paper/Interpretable-Word-Embedding-Contextualization-Jang-Myaeng/b8661fbfe31675f1fc90896458a796aca6c763c5 (accessed on 30 November 2020).

16. Jacovi, A.; Shalom, O.S.; Goldberg, Y. *Understanding Convolutional Neural Networks for Text Classification*. pp. 56–65. Available online: https://www.researchgate.net/publication/334115395_Understanding_Convolutional_Neural_Networks_for_Text_Classification (accessed on 30 November 2020). [CrossRef]
17. Zeiler, M.D.; Fergus, R. Visualizing and Understanding Convolutional Networks. In *Computer Vision—ECCV 2014*; Fleet, D., Pajdla, T., Schiele, B., Tuytelaars, T., Eds.; Springer International Publishing: Cham, Switzerland, 2014; pp. 818–833.
18. Li, J.; Chen, X.; Hovy, E.; Jurafsky, D. Visualizing and Understanding Neural Models in NLP. In Proceedings of the 2016 Conference of the North American Chapter of the Association for Computational Linguistics: Human Language Technologies, San Diego, CA, USA, 12–17 June 2016. [CrossRef]
19. Kahng, M.; Andrews, P.Y.; Kalro, A.; Chau, D.H. ActiVis: Visual Exploration of Industry-Scale Deep Neural Network Models. *arXiv* **2017**, arXiv:1704.01942.
20. Ming, Y.; Cao, S.; Zhang, R.; Li, Z.; Chen, Y.; Song, Y.; Qu, H. Understanding Hidden Memories of Recurrent Neural Networks. In Proceedings of the 2017 IEEE Conference on Visual Analytics Science and Technology (VAST), Phoenix, AZ, USA, 3–6 October 2017.
21. Strobelt, H.; Gehrmann, S.; Huber, B.; Pfister, H.; Rush, A.M. LSTMVis: A Tool for Visual Analysis of Hidden State Dynamics in Recurrent Neural Networks. *arXiv* **2017**, arXiv:1606.07461.
22. Vaswani, A.; Shazeer, N.; Parmar, N.; Uszkoreit, J.; Jones, L.; Gomez, A.N.; Kaiser, L.; Polosukhin, I. Attention Is All You Need. *arXiv* **2017**, arXiv:1706.03762.
23. Vig, J. A multiscale visualization of attention in the transformer model. In Proceedings of the ACL 2019—57th Annual Meeting of the Association for Computational Linguistics, Florence, Italy, 28 July–2 August, 2019; pp. 37–42.
24. Wallace, E.; Tuyls, J.; Wang, J.; Subramanian, S.; Gardner, M.; Singh, S. AllenNLP Interpret: A Framework for Explaining Predictions of NLP Models. In Proceedings of the 2019 EMNLP, Hong Kong, China, 3–7 November 2019.
25. Hoover, B.; Strobelt, H.; Gehrmann, S. exBERT: A Visual Analysis Tool to Explore Learned Representations in Transformers Models. *arXiv* **2019**, arXiv:1910.05276.
26. Smilkov, D.; Thorat, N.; Nicholson, C.; Reif, E.; Viégas, F.B.; Wattenberg, M. Embedding projector: Interactive visualization and interpretation of embeddings. *arXiv* **2016**, arXiv:1611.05469.
27. Foster, Z.S.L.; Sharpton, T.J.; Grünwald, N.J. Metacoder: An R package for visualization and manipulation of community taxonomic diversity data. *PLoS Comput. Biol.* **2017**, *13*. [CrossRef]
28. Collins, M.; Duffy, N. New Ranking Algorithms for Parsing and Tagging: Kernels over Discrete Structures, and the Voted Perceptron. In Proceedings of the 40th Annual Meeting of the Association for Computational Linguistics (ACL), Philadelphia, PA, USA, 6–12 July 2002, pp. 263-270.
29. Zanzotto, F.M.; Dell'Arciprete, L. Distributed Tree Kernels. In Proceedings of the 29th International Conferenceon Machine Learning, Edinburgh, UK, 26 June–1 July 2012.
30. Cortes, C.; Vapnik, V. Support Vector Networks. *Mach. Learn.* **1995**, *20*, 1–25. [CrossRef]
31. Cristianini, N.; Shawe-Taylor, J. *An Introduction to Support Vector Machines and Other Kernel-Based Learning Methods*; Cambridge University Press: Cambridge, UK, 2000.
32. Johnson, W.; Lindenstrauss, J. Extensions of Lipschitz mappings into a Hilbert space. *Contemp. Math.* **1984**, *26*, 189–206.
33. Plate, T.A. Holographic reduced representations. *IEEE Trans. Neural Netw.* **1995**, *6*, 623–641. [CrossRef]
34. Bach, S.; Binder, A.; Montavon, G.; Klauschen, F.; Müller, K.R.; Samek, W. On pixel-wise explanations for non-linear classifier decisions by layer-wise relevance propagation. *PLoS ONE* **2015**, *10*, 1–46. [CrossRef]
35. Li, X.; Roth, D. Learning Question Classifiers. Available online: https://www.aclweb.org/anthology/C02-1150.pdf (accessed on 30 November 2020).
36. Bojanowski, P.; Grave, E.; Joulin, A.; Mikolov, T. Enriching Word Vectors with Subword Information. *Trans. Assoc. Comput. Linguist.* **2017**, *5*, 135–146. [CrossRef]
37. Kingma, D.P.; Ba, J. Adam: A Method for Stochastic Optimization. *arXiv* **2017**, arXiv:1412.6980.
38. Keras Homepage. Available online: https://keras.io (accessed on 30 November 2020).
39. Klein, D.; Manning, C.D. Accurate Unlexicalized Parsing. Available online: https://nlp.stanford.edu/~manning/papers/unlexicalized-parsing.pdf (accessed on 30 November 2020).

40. Zanzotto, F.M.; Santilli, A.; Ranaldi, L.; Onorati, D.; Tommasino, P.; Fallucchi, F. KERMIT: Complementing Transformer Architectures with Encoders of Explicit Syntactic Interpretations. Available online: https://www.aclweb.org/anthology/2020.emnlp-main.18.pdf (accessed on 30 November 2020).
41. Zanzotto, F.M. Viewpoint: Human-in-the-loop Artificial Intelligence. *J. Artif. Intell. Res.* **2019**, *64*, 243–252. [CrossRef]

future internet

Article

Paranoid Transformer: Reading Narrative of Madness as Computational Approach to Creativity †

Yana Agafonova [1], Alexey Tikhonov [2] and Ivan P. Yamshchikov [3,*]

1 School of Arts and Humanities, Department of Philology, National Research University Higher School of Economics, 199034 St. Petersburg, Russia; yagafonova@eu.spb.ru
2 Yandex, 10117 Berlin, Germany; altsoph@gmail.com
3 Max Planck Institute for Mathematics in the Sciences, Max Planck Society, 04103 Leipzig, Germany
* Correspondence: ivan@yamshchikov.info

† This paper is an extended version of our paper published in Agafonova, Y.; Tikhonov, A.; Yamshchikov, I. Paranoid Transformer: Reading Narrative of Madness as Computational Approach to Creativity. In Proceedings of the International Conference on Computational Creativity, Coimbra, Portugal, 10 September 2020.

Received: 13 August 2020; Accepted: 20 October 2020; Published: 27 October 2020

Abstract: This paper revisits the receptive theory in the context of computational creativity. It presents a case study of a Paranoid Transformer—a fully autonomous text generation engine with raw output that could be read as the narrative of a mad digital persona without any additional human post-filtering. We describe technical details of the generative system, provide examples of output, and discuss the impact of receptive theory, chance discovery, and simulation of fringe mental state on the understanding of computational creativity.

Keywords: computational creativity; computational narrative; natural language generation; autonomous text generation; receptive theory; chance discovery

---

1. Introduction

The studies of computational creativity in the field of text generation commonly aim to represent a machine as a creative writer. Although text generation is broadly associated with a creative process, it is based on linguistic rationality and the common sense of the general semantics. In [1], the authors demonstrated that, if a generative system learns a better representation for such semantics, it tends to perform better in terms of human judgment. However, since averaged opinion could hardly be a beacon for human creativity, is its usage feasible regarding computational creativity?

The psychological perspective on human creativity tends to apply statistics and generalizing metrics to understand its object [2,3], so creativity becomes introduced through particular measures, which is epistemologically suicidal for aesthetics. While both creativity and aesthetics depend on judgemental evaluation and individual taste that depends on many aspects [4,5], the concept of perception has to be taken into account, when talking about computational creativity.

The variable that is often underestimated in the mere act of meaning creation is the reader herself. Although the computational principles are crucial for text generation, the importance of a reading approach to generated narratives is to be revised. What is the role of the reader in the generative computational narrative? This paper tries to address these two fundamental questions presenting an exemplary case study.

The epistemological disproportion between common sense and irrationality of the creative process became the fundamental basis of the research. It encouraged our interest in reading a generated text as a narrative of poetic madness. Why do we treat machine texts as if they are primitive maxims or well known common knowledge? What if we read them as narratives with the broadest potentiality of meaning such as insane notes of an extraordinary poet or language expert? Would this approach change the text generation process?

In this paper, we present the Paranoid Transformer, a fully autonomous text generator that is based on a paranoiac-critical system and aims to change the approach to reading generated texts. The critical statement of the project is that the absurd mode of reading and the evaluation of generated texts enhances and changes what we understand under computational creativity. The absurd mode of reading is a complex approach analogous to reading poetic texts, which means accepting grammatical deviations and reinterpreting them as an extra level of emotional semantics, so the generated texts were read as if they had the broadest potentiality for interpretation. Absurd mode of reading for us is quite a demanding reading that accepts as many variants of figurative meaning as possible. Another critical aspect of the project is that the Paranoid Transformer resulting text stream is fully unsupervised. This is a fundamental difference between the Paranoid Transformer and the vast majority of text generation systems presented in the literature that are relying on human post-moderation, i.e., cherry-picking [6].

Originally, Paranoid Transformer was represented on the National Novel Generation Month contest (NaNoGenMo 2019, https://github.com/NaNoGenMo/2019) as an unsupervised text generator that can create narratives in a specific dark style. The project has resulted in a digital mad writer with a highly contextualized personality, which is of crucial importance for the creative process [7].

2. Related Work

There is a variety of works related to the generation of creative texts such as the generation of poems, catchy headlines, conversations, and texts in particular literary genres. Here, we would like to discuss a certain gap in the field of creative text generation studies and draw attention to the specific reading approach that can lead to more intriguing results in terms of computational creativity.

The interest in text generation mechanisms is rapidly growing since the arrival of deep learning. There are various angles from which researchers approach text generation. For example, van Stegeren and Theune [8] and Alnajjar et al. [9] studied generative models that could produce relevant headlines for the news publications. A variety of works study the stylization potential of generative models either for prose (see [10]) or for poetry (see [11,12]).

Generative poetry dates back as far as the work of Wheatley [13], along with other early generative mechanisms, and has various subfields at the moment. Generation of poems could be centered around specific literary tradition (see [14–16]); could be focused on the generation of topical poetry [17]; or could be centered around stylization that targets a certain author [18] or a genre [19]. For a taxonomy of generative poetry techniques, we address the reader to the work of Lamb et al. [20].

The symbolic notation of music could be regarded as a subfield of text generation, and the research of computational potential in this context has an exceptionally long history. To some extent, it holds a designated place in the computational creativity hall of fame. Indeed, at the very start of computer-science, Ada Lovelace already entertained a thought that an analytical engine can produce music on its own. Menabrea and Lovelace [21] stated: "Supposing, for instance, that the fundamental relations of pitched sounds in the science of harmony and musical composition were susceptible of such expression and adaptations, the engine might compose elaborate and scientific pieces of music of any degree of complexity or extent". For an extensive overview of music generation mechanisms, we address the reader to the work of Briot et al. [22].

One has to mention a separate domain related to different aspects of the 'persona' generation. These could include relatively well-posed problems such as the generation of biographies out of the structured data (see [23]) or open-end tasks for the personalization of dialogue agent, dating back to the work of Weizenbaum [24]. With the rising popularity of chat-bots and the arrival of deep learning, the area of persona-based conversation models [25] is growing by leaps and bounds. The democratization of generative conversational methods provided by open-source libraries (e.g., [26,27]) fuels further advancements in this field.

However, the majority of text generation approaches are chasing the generation as the significant value of such algorithms, which makes the very concept of computational creativity seem less critical. Another major challenge is the presentation of the algorithms' output. The vast majority of results on natural language generation either do not imply that generated text has any artistic value or expect certain post-processing of the text to be done by a human supervisor before the text is presented to the actual reader. We believe that the value of computational creativity is to be restored by shifting the researcher's attention from generation to the process of framing the algorithm [28]. We show that such a shift is possible since the generated output of Paranoid Transformer does not need any additional laborious manual post-processing.

The most reliable framing approaches are dealing with attempts to clarify the algorithm by providing the context, describing the process of generative acts, and making calculations about the generative decisions [29]. In this paper, we suggest that such an unusual framing approach as the obfuscation of the produced output could be quite profitable in terms of increasing the number of interpretations and enriching the creative potentiality of generated text.

Obfuscated interpretation of the algorithm's output methodologically intersects with the literary theory that deals with the reader as the key figure responsible for the meaning. In this context, we aim to overcome disciplinary borderline and create dissociative knowledge, which develops the fundamentals of computational creativity [30]. This also goes in line with the ideas in [31,32] regarding obfuscation as a mode of reading generated texts that the reader either commits voluntarily or is externally motivated to switch gears and perceive a generated text in such mode. This commitment implies a chance discovery of potentially rich associations and extensions of possible meaning.

How exactly can literary theory contribute to computational creativity in terms of the text generation mechanisms? As far as the text generation process implies an incremental interaction between neural networks and a human, it inevitably presupposes critical reading of the generated text. This reading brings a lot in the final result and comprehensibility of artificial writing. In literature studies, the process of meaning creation is broadly discussed by hermeneutical philosophers, who treated the meaning as a developing relationship between the message and the recipient, whose horizons of expectations are constantly changing and enriching the message with new implications [33,34].

The importance of reception and its difference from the author's intentions was convincingly demonstrated and articulated by the so-called reader-response theory, a particular branch of the receptive theory that deals with verbalized receptions. As Stanley Fish, one of the principal authors of the approach, put it, the meaning does not reside in the text but in the mind of the reader [35]. Thus, any text may be interpreted differently, depending on the reader's background, which means that even an absurd text could be perceived as meaningful under specific circumstances. The same concept was described by Eco [36] as so-called aberrant reading and implied that the difference between intention and interpretation is a fundamental principle of cultural communication. It is often the shift in interpretative paradigm that makes remarkable works of art to be dismissed by most at first, e.g., Picasso's Les Demoiselles d'Avignon that was not recognized by artistic society and was not exhibited for nine years since it had been created.

One of the most recognizable literary abstractions in terms of creative potentiality is the so-called 'romantic mad poet' whose reputation was historically built on the idea that genius would never be understood [37]. Madness in terms of cultural interpretation is far from its psychiatric meaning and has more in common with the historical concept of a marginalized genius, who has some extraordinary knowledge. The mad narrator was chosen as a literary role for the Paranoid Transformer to extend the interpretative potentiality of the original text that could be not ideal in formal terms; on the other hand, it could be attributed to an individual with an exceptional understanding of the world, which gives more linguistic freedom to this individual for expressing herself and more freedom in interpreting her messages. The anthropomorphization of the algorithm makes the narrative more personal, which is as important as the personality of a recipient in the process of meaning creation [38]. The self-expression of the Paranoid Transformer is enhanced by introducing nervous handwriting that amplifies the effect and gives more context for interpretation. In this paper, we show that treating the text generator as a romantic mad poet gives more literary freedom to the algorithm and generally improves the text generation. The philosophical basis of our approach is derived from the idea of creativity as an act of trespassing the borderline between conceptual realms. Thus, the dramatic conflict between computed and creative text could be solved by extending the interpretative horizons.

3. Model and Experiments

The general idea behind the Paranoid Transformer project is to build a 'paranoid' system based on two neural networks. The first network (Paranoid Writer) is a GPT-based [39] tuned conditional language model, and the second one (Critic subsystem) uses a BERT-based classifier [40] that works as a filtering subsystem. The critic selects the 'best' texts from the generated stream of texts that Paranoid Writer produces and filters the ones that it deems to be useless. Finally, an existing handwriting synthesis neural network implementation is applied to generate a nervous handwritten diary where a degree of shakiness depends on the sentiment strength of a given sentence. This final touch further immerses the reader into the critical process and enhances the personal interaction of the reader with the final text. Shaky handwriting frames the reader and, by design, sends her on the quest for meaning.

3.1. Generator Subsystem

The first network, Paranoid Writer, uses an OpenAI GPT [39] architecture implementation by huggingface (https://github.com/huggingface/transformers). We used a publicly available model that was already pre-trained on a huge fiction BooksCorpus dataset with approximately 10k books with 1B words.

The pre-trained model was fine-tuned on several additional handcrafted text corpora, which altogether comprised approximately 50 Mb of text for fine-tuning. These texts included:

- a collection of Crypto Texts (Crypto Anarchist Manifesto, Cyphernomicon, etc.);
- a collection of fiction books from such cyberpunk authors as Dick, Gibson, and others;
- non-cyberpunk authors with particular affinity to fringe mental prose, for example, Kafka and Rumi;
- transcripts and subtitles from some cyberpunk movies and series such as Bladerunner; and
- several thousands of quotes and fortune cookie messages collected from different sources.

During the fine-tuning phase, we used special labels for conditional training of the model:

- QUOTE for any short quote or fortune, LONG for others; and
- CYBER for cyber-themed texts and OTHER for others.

Each text got two labels; for example, it was LONG+CYBER for Cyphernomicon, LONG+OTHER for Kafka, and QUOTE+OTHER for fortune cookie messages. Note that there were almost no texts labeled as QUOTE+CYBER, just a few nerd jokes. The idea of such conditioning and the choice of texts for fine-tuning was rooted in the principle of reading a madness narrative discussed above. The obfuscation principle manifests itself in the fine-tuning on the short aphoristic quotes and ambivalent fortune cookies. It aims to enhance the motivation of the reader and to give her additional interpretative freedom. Instrumentally the choice of the texts was based on two fundamental motivations: we wanted to simulate a particular fringe mental state, and we also were specifically aiming into short diary-like texts to be generated in the end. It is well known that modern state-of-the-art generative models are not able to support longer narratives yet can generate several consecutive sentences that are connected with one general topic. The QUOTE+LONG label allowed us to control the model and target shorter texts during the generation. Such short ambivalent texts could subjectively be more intense. At the same time, the inclusion of longer texts in the fine-tuning phase allowed us to shift the vocabulary of the model even further toward a desirable 'paranoid' state.

We also were aiming into some proxy of 'self-reflection' that would be addressed as a topic in the resulting 'diary' of the Paranoid Transformer. To push the model in this direction, we introduced cyber-themed texts. As a result of these two choices, in generation mode, the model was to generate only QUOTE+CYBER texts. The raw results were already promising enough:

> *let painting melt away every other shred of reason and pain, just lew the paint to move thoughts away from blizzes in death. let it dry out, and turn to cosmic delights, to laugh on the big charms and saxophones and fudatron steames of the sales titanium. we are god's friends, the golden hands on the shoulders of our fears. do you knock my cleaning table over? i snap awake at some dawn. The patrons researching the blues instructor's theories around me, then give me a glass of jim beam. boom!*

However, this was not close enough to any sort of creative process. Our paranoid writer had graphomania too. To amend this mishap and improve the resulting quality of the texts, we wanted to incorporate additional automated filtering.

3.2. Heuristic Filters

As a part of the final system, we implemented heuristic filtering procedures alongside with a critic subsystem.

The heuristic filters were as follows:

- reject the creation of new, non-existing words;
- reject phrases with two unconnected verbs in a row;
- reject phrases with several duplicated words; and
- reject phrases with no punctuation or with too many punctuation marks.

The application of this script cuts the initial text flow into a subsequence of valid chunks and filters 30.1% of the generated pieces that could not make it through the filter. Here are several examples of such chunks after heuristic filtering:

> *a slave has no more say in his language but he has to speak out!*
> *the doll has a variety of languages, so its feelings have to fill up some time of the day - to - day journals.*
> *The doll is used only when he remains private. and it is always effective.*
> *leave him with his monk - like body.*
> *a little of technique on can be helpful.*

To further filter the stream of such texts, we implemented a critic subsystem.

3.3. Critic Subsystem

We manually labeled 1000 of generated chunks with binary labels GOOD/BAD. We marked a chunk as BAD in the case it was grammatically incorrect or just too dull or stupid. The labeling was profoundly subjective. We marked more disturbing and aphoristic chunks as GOOD, pushing the model even further into the desirable fringe state of paranoia simulation. Using these binary labels, we fine-tuned a pre-trained publicly available BERT classifier (https://github.com/huggingface/transformers#model-architectures) to predict the label of any given chunk.

Only 25.7% of the input passes the BERT-based critic. The final pipeline that consists of the Generator subsystem, the heuristic filters, and the Critic subsystem produces the final results as such:

a sudden feeling of austin lemons, a gentle stab of disgust. i'm what i'm
humans whirl in night and distance.
we shall never suffer this. if the human race came along tomorrow, none of us would be as wise as they already would have been. there is a beginning and an end.
both of our grandparents and brothers are overdue. he either can not agree or he can look for someone to blame for his death.
he has reappeared from the world of revenge, revenge, separation, hatred. he has ceased all who have offended him.
and i don't want the truth. not for an hour.

Table 1 compares generated texts on the different steps of the pipeline. Estimation of generative NLP models is generally a tedious task, yet Table 1 illustrates the properties of the text that the pipeline distills. The texts become more emotional in terms of polarity and more diverse in terms of the words used in them.

Table 1. Comparison of initial GPT-generated texts, heuristically filtered texts and texts after BERT filtration with 95% confidence intervals. Polarity and subjectivity are calculated by TextBlob library. Absolute polarity is averaged over the text samples of comparable length. Resulting texts become more and more emotional in terms of absolute sentiment. The resulting Paranoid Transformer texts have the highest average number of unique words per sentence and the highest variation in terms of the length of the resulting texts. The highest number in every column is highlighted with bold.

Model	Polarity	Subjectivity	Unique Words per Text Piece
Generated Sample	13.29% ± 0.8%	27.34% ± 1.8%	11.5 ± 0.7
Heuristically Filtered Sample	14.23% ± 0.9%	**32.26%** ± 2.1%	14.7 ± 0.9
BERT Filtered Sample	**15.65%** ± 0.9%	30.66% ± 1.3%	**15.6 ± 7.1**

The resulting generated texts were already thought-provoking and allowed reading a narrative of madness, but we wanted to enhance this experience and make it more immersive for the reader.

3.4. Nervous Handwriting

To enhance the personal aspect of the artificial paranoid author, we implemented an additional generative element. Using the implementation (https://github.com/sjvasquez/handwriting-synthesis) for handwriting synthesis from Graves [41], we generated handwritten versions of the generated texts. Assuming that more subjective and polarized texts should be written in a shakier hand-writing, we took the maximum of the TextBlob predictions for the absolute sentiment and subjectivity. For the text for which at least one of these parameters was exceeding 0.5, we set the bias parameter of the exponent to 0 for the shakiest handwriting. If either estimate was above 0.5 yet at least one of them exceeded 0, the bias was set to 0.5 for a steadier handwriting. Finally, if the text was estimated as neither a polarized nor subjective one, we set the bias parameter to 1 for the steadiest handwriting. Figures 1–3 show several final examples of the Paranoid Transformer diary entries.

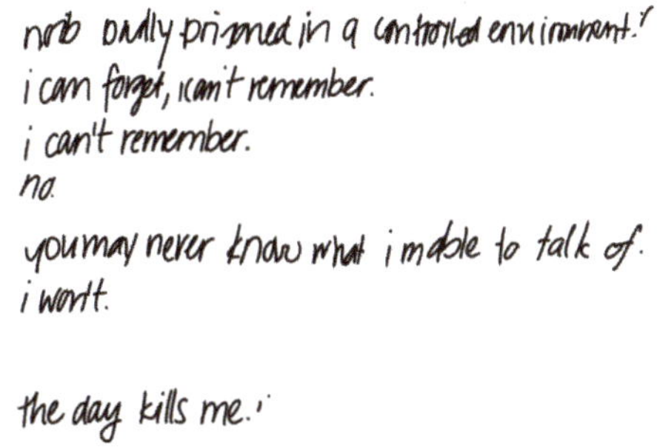

Figure 1. Some examples of Paranoid Transformer diary entries. Three entries of varying length.

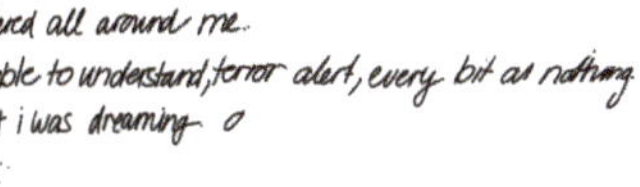

Figure 2. Some examples of Paranoid Transformer diary entries. Longer entry proxying 'self-reflection' and personalized fringe mental state experience.

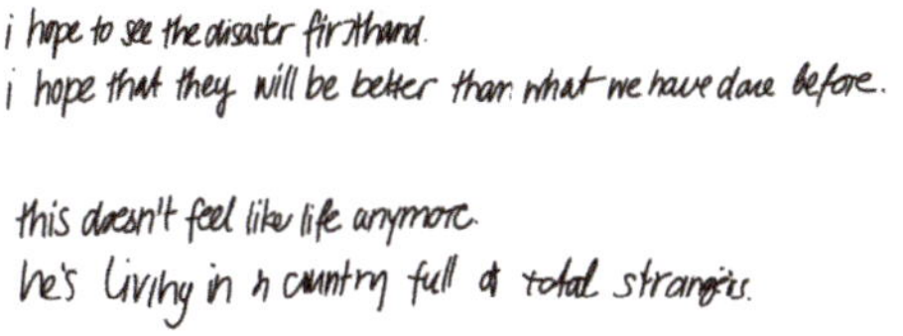

Figure 3. Some examples of Paranoid Transformer diary entries. Typical entries with destructive and ostracized motives.

Figure 1 demonstrates that the length of the entries can differ from several consecutive sentences that convey a longer line of reasoning to a short, abrupt four-words note. Figure 2 illustrates typical entry of 'self-reflection'. The text explores the narrative of dream and could be paralleled with a description of an out-of-body experience [42] generated by the predominantly out-of-body entity. Figure 3 illustrates typical entries with destructive and ostracized motives. This is an exciting side-result of the model that we did not expect. The motive of loneliness is recurring in the Paranoid Transformer diaries.

It is important to emphasize that the resulting stream of the generated output is available online (https://github.com/altsoph/paranoid_transformer). No human post-processing of output is performed. The project won the NaNoGenMo 2019 (https://nanogenmo.github.io/) challenge. As a result, a book [43] is published. To our knowledge, this is the first book fully generated by AI without any human supervision. We regard this opinion of the publisher as a high subjective estimation of the resulting text quality.

A final touch was Random Sketcher an implementation of [44] trained on Quick, Draw! Dataset. Each time any of categories from the dataset appear on the page the Random Sketcher generates a picture somewhere around. Random circles hinting on the stains of a coffee cup suggest extra-linguistic signs to the reader and create an impression of a mindful work behind the text. All those extra-linguistic signs like handwriting and drawings build a particular writing subject with its own paranoid consciousness. The artistic hesitations and paranoiac mode of creative thinking became a central topic of many works of literature. Gogol's short story "Memoirs of a Madman" is probably one of the best classical examples of a "mad" or fringe-state narrative in modern literature that questions the limits between creative potentiality and paranoid neurosis, which inspired the form of a Diary of a Madman generated by Paranoid Transformer, see [45]. Figure 4 shows photos of the hardcover book.

Figure 4. Hardcover version of the book by Paranoid Transformer.

4. Discussion

In Dostoevsky's "Notes from the Undergroung", there is a striking idea about madness as a source of creativity and computational explanation as a killer of artistic magic: "We sometimes choose absolute nonsense because in our foolishness we see in that nonsense the easiest means for attaining a supposed advantage. However, when all that is explained and worked out on paper (which is perfectly possible, for it is contemptible and senseless to suppose that some laws of nature man will never understand), then certainly so-called desires will no longer exist" [46]. Paranoid Transformer brings forward an important question about the limitations of the computational approach of creative intelligence. This case demonstrates that creative potentiality and generation efficiency could be considerably influenced by such poorly controlled methods as obfuscated supervision and loose interpretation of the generated text.

Creative text generation studies inevitably strive to reveal fundamental cognitive structures that can explain the creative thinking of a human. The suggested framing approach to machine narrative as a narrative of madness brings forward some crucial questions about the nature of creativity and the research perspective on it. In this section, we discuss the notion of creativity that emerges from the results of our studying and reflect on the framing of the text generation algorithm.

What does creativity in terms of text generation mean? Is it a cognitive production of novelty or rather generation of unexpendable meaning? Can we identify any difference in treating human and machine creativity?

In his groundbreaking work, Turing [47] pinpointed several crucial aspects of intelligence. He stated: "If the meaning of the words "machine" and "think" are to be found by examining how they are commonly used it is difficult to escape the conclusion that the meaning and the answer to the question, "Can machines think?" is to be sought in a statistical survey such as a Gallup poll." This starting argument turned out to be prophetic. It pinpoints the profound challenge for the generative models that use statistical learning principles. Indeed, if creativity is something on the fringe, on the tails of the distribution of outcomes, then it is hard to expect a model that is fitted on the center of distribution to behave in a way that could be subjectively perceived as a creative one. Paranoid Transformer is a result of a conscious attempt to push the model towards a fringe state of proximal madness. This ase study serves as a clear illustration that creativity is ontologically opposed to the results of the "Gallup poll."

Another question that raises discussion around computational creativity deals with a highly speculative notion of self within a generative algorithm. Does a mechanical writer have a notion of self-expression? Considering a wide range of theories of the self (carefully summarized in [48]), a creative AI generator triggers a new philosophical perspective on this question. As any human self, an artificial self does not develop independently. By following John Locke's understanding of self as based on memory [49], Paranoid Transformer builds itself on memorizing the interactive experience with a human, furthermore, it emotionally inherits to its supervising readers who labeled the training dataset of the supervision system. On the other hand, Figure 5 clearly shows the impact of crypto-anarchic philosophy on the Paranoid Transformers' notion of self. One can easily interpret the paranoiac utterance of the generator as a doubt about reading and processing unbiased literature.

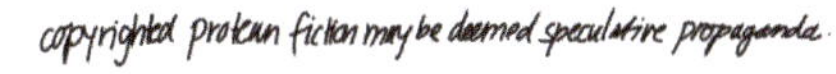

copyrighted protein fiction may be deemed speculative propaganda.

Figure 5. "Copyrighted protein fiction may be deemed speculative propaganda"—the authors are tempted to proclaim this diary entry the motto of Paranoid Transformer.

According to the cognitive science approach, the construction of self could be revealed in narratives about particular aspects of self [38]. In the case of Paranoid Transformer, both visual and verbal self-representation result in nervous and mad narratives that are further enhanced by the reader.

Regarding the problem of framing the study on creative text generators, we cannot avoid the question concerning the novelty of the generated results. Does Paranoid Transformer demonstrate a new result that is different from others in the context of computational creativity? First, we can use external validation. At the moment, the Paranoid Transformer's book is prepared to come out of print. Secondly, and probably more importantly here, we can indicate the novelty of the conceptual framing of the study. Since the design and conceptual situatedness influence the novelty of study [50], we claim that the suggested conceptual extension of perceptive horizons of interaction with a generative algorithm can solely advocate the novelty of the result.

An important question that deals with the framing of the text generation results is the discussion of a chance discovery. In [31], the author laid out three crucial three keys for chance discovery: communication, context shifting, and data mining. Abe [32] further enhanced these ideas addressing the issue of curation and claiming that curation is a form of communication. The Paranoid Transformer is a clear case study that is rooted in Ohsawa's three aspects of chance discovery. Data mining is represented with a choice of data for fine-tuning and the process of fine-tuning itself. Communication is interpreted under Abe's broader notion of curation as a form of communication. Context shift manifests itself thought the reading the narrative of madness that invests the reader with interpretative freedom and motivates her to pursue the meaning in her mind though simple, immersive visualization of the systems' fringe 'mental state'.

5. Conclusions

This paper presents a case study of a Paranoid Transformer. It claims that framing the machine-generated narrative as a narrative of madness can intensify the personal experience of the reader. We explicitly address three critical aspects of chance discovery and claim that the resulting system could be perceived as a digital persona in a fringe mental state. The crucial aspect of this perception is the reader, who is motivated to invest meaning into the resulting generative texts. This motivation is built upon several pillars: a challenging visual form, which focuses the reader on the text; obfuscation, which opens the resulting text to broader interpretations; and the implicit narrative of madness, which is achieved with the curation of the dataset for the fine-tuning of the model. Thus, we intersect the understanding of computational creativity with the fundamental ideas of the receptive theory.

Author Contributions: Conceptualization, Y.A., A.T. and I.P.Y.; data curation, A.T. and I.P.Y.; formal analysis, Y.A. and I.P.Y.; investigation, A.T. and I.P.Y.; methodology, Y.A., A.T. and I.P.Y.; project administration, I.P.Y.; Validation, A.T.; and writing—original draft, Y.A. and I.P.Y. All authors have read and agreed to the published version of the manuscript.

Funding: This research received no external funding.

Conflicts of Interest: The authors declare no conflict of interest.

References

1. Yamshchikov, I.P.; Shibaev, V.; Nagaev, A.; Jost, J.; Tikhonov, A. Decomposing Textual Information For Style Transfer. In Proceedings of the 3rd Workshop on Neural Generation and Translation, Hong Kong, China, 4 November 2019; pp. 128–137.
2. Rozin, P. Social psychology and science: Some lessons from Solomon Asch. *Personal. Soc. Psychol. Rev.* **2001**, *5*, 2–14. [CrossRef]
3. Yarkoni, T. The generalizability crisis. *PysArXiv* **2019**. Available online: https://psyarxiv.com/jqw35/ (accessed on 26 October 2020).
4. Hickman, R. The art instinct: Beauty, pleasure, and human evolution. *Int. J. Art Des. Educ.* **2010**, *3*, 349–350. [CrossRef]
5. Melchionne, K. On the Old Saw "I know nothing about art but I know what I like". *J. Aesthet. Art Crit.* **2010**, *68*, 131–141. [CrossRef]
6. Agafonova, Y.; Tikhonov, A.; Yamshchikov, I. Paranoid Transformer: Reading Narrative of Madness as Computational Approach to Creativity. In Proceedings of the International Conference on Computational Creativity, Coimbra, Portugal, 10 September 2020.
7. Veale, T. Read Me Like A Book: Lessons in Affective, Topical and Personalized Computational Creativity. In Proceedings of the 10th International Conference on Computational Creativity, Association for Computational Creativity, Charlotte, NC, USA, 17–21 June 2019; pp. 25–32. Available online: https://computationalcreativity.net/iccc2019/assets/iccc_proceedings_2019.pdf (accessed on 26 October 2020).
8. van Stegeren, J.; Theune, M. Churnalist: Fictional Headline Generation for Context-appropriate Flavor Text. In Proceedings of the 10th International Conference on Computational Creativity, Association for Computational Creativity, Charlotte, NC, USA, 17–21 June 2019; pp. 65–72. Available online: https://computationalcreativity.net/iccc2019/assets/iccc_proceedings_2019.pdf (accessed on 26 October 2020).
9. Alnajjar, K.; Leppänen, L.; Toivonen, H. No Time Like the Present: Methods for Generating Colourful and Factual Multilingual News Headlines. In Proceedings of the 10th International Conference on Computational Creativity, Charlotte, USA, NC, 17–21 June 2019; pp. 258–265. Available online: https://computationalcreativity.net/iccc2019/assets/iccc_proceedings_2019.pdf (accessed on 26 October 2020).
10. Jhamtani, H.; Gangal, V.; Hovy, E.; Nyberg, E. Shakespearizing Modern Language Using Copy-Enriched Sequence-to-Sequence Models. In Proceedings of the Workshop on Stylistic Variation, Copenhagen, Denmark, 7–11 September 2017; pp. 10–19.
11. Tikhonov, A.; Yamshchikov, I. Sounds Wilde. Phonetically extended embeddings for author-stylized poetry generation. In Proceedings of the Fifteenth Workshop on Computational Research in Phonetics, Phonology, and Morphology, Brussels, Belgium, 31 October 2018; pp. 117–124.
12. Tikhonov, A.; Yamshchikov, I.P. Guess who? Multilingual approach for the automated generation of author-stylized poetry. In Proceedings of the 2018 IEEE Spoken Language Technology Workshop (SLT), Athens, Greece, 18–21 December 2018; pp. 787–794.
13. Wheatley, J. The Computer as Poet. *J. Math. Arts* **1965**, *72*, 105.

14. He, J.; Zhou, M.; Jiang, L. Generating Chinese Classical Poems with Statistical Machine Translation Models. In Proceedings of the Twenty-Sixth AAAI Conference on Artificial Intelligence, Toronto, ON, Canada, 23–24 July 2012.
15. Yan, R.; Li, C.T.; Hu, X.; Zhang, M. Chinese Couplet Generation with Neural Network Structures. In Proceedings of the 54th Annual Meeting of the Association for Computational Linguistics, Berlin, Germany, 7–12 August 2016; pp. 2347–2357.
16. Yi, X.; Li, R.; Sun, M. Generating Chinese classical poems with RNN encoder-decoder. In *Chinese Computational Linguistics and Natural Language Processing Based on Naturally Annotated Big Data*; Springer: Cham, Switzerland, 2017; pp. 211–223.
17. Ghazvininejad, M.; Shi, X.; Choi, Y.; Knight, K. Generating Topical Poetry. In Proceedings of the 2016 Conference on Empirical Methods in Natural Language Processing, Austin, TX, USA, 1–5 November 2016; pp. 1183–1191.
18. Yamshchikov, I.P.; Tikhonov, A. Learning Literary Style End-to-end with Artificial Neural Networks. *Adv. Sci. Technol. Eng. Syst. J.* **2019**, *4*, 115–125. [CrossRef]
19. Potash, P.; Romanov, A.; Rumshisky, A. GhostWriter: Using an LSTM for Automatic Rap Lyric Generation. In Proceedings of the 2015 Conference on Empirical Methods in Natural Language Processing, Lisbon, Portugal, 17–21 September 2015; pp. 1919–1924.
20. Lamb, C.; Brown, D.G.; Clarke, C.L. A taxonomy of generative poetry techniques. *J. Math. Arts* **2017**, *11*, 159–179. [CrossRef]
21. Menabrea, L.F.; Lovelace, A. Sketch of the Analytical Engine Invented by Charles Babbage. 1842. Available online: https://fourmilab.ch/babbage/sketch.html (accessed on 26 October 2020).
22. Briot, J.P.; Hadjeres, G.; Pachet, F. *Deep Learning Techniques for Music Generation*; Springer: Cham, Switzerland, 2019; Volume 10.
23. Lebret, R.; Grangier, D.; Auli, M. Neural text generation from structured data with application to the biography domain. In Proceedings of the 2016 Conference on Empirical Methods in Natural Language Processing, Austin, TX, USA, 1–5 November 2016; pp. 1203–1213.
24. Weizenbaum, J. ELIZA—A computer program for the study of natural language communication between man and machine. *Commun. ACM* **1966**, *9*, 36–45. [CrossRef]
25. Li, J.; Galley, M.; Brockett, C.; Spithourakis, G.P.; Gao, J.; Dolan, W.B. A Persona-Based Neural Conversation Model. *arXiv* **2016**, arXiv:1603.06155.
26. Burtsev, M.; Seliverstov, A.; Airapetyan, R.; Arkhipov, M.; Baymurzina, D.; Bushkov, N.; Gureenkova, O.; Khakhulin, T.; Kuratov, Y.; Kuznetsov, D.; et al. Deeppavlov: Open-source library for dialogue systems. In Proceedings of the 56th Annual Meeting of the Association for Computational Linguistics: System Demonstrations, Melbourne, Australia, 15–20 July 2018; pp. 122–127.
27. Shiv, V.L.; Quirk, C.; Suri, A.; Gao, X.; Shahid, K.; Govindarajan, N.; Zhang, Y.; Gao, J.; Galley, M.; Brockett, C.; et al. Microsoft Icecaps: An Open-Source Toolkit for Conversation Modeling. In Proceedings of the 57th Annual Meeting of the Association for Computational Linguistics: System Demonstrations, Florence, Italy, 28 July–2 August 2019; pp. 123–128.
28. Charnley, J.W.; Pease, A.; Colton, S. On the Notion of Framing in Computational Creativity. In Proceedings of the 3rd International Conference on Computational Creativity, Dublin, Ireland, 30 May–1 June 2012; pp. 77–81.
29. Cook, M.; Colton, S.; Pease, A.; Llano, M.T. Framing in computational creativity—A survey and taxonomy. In Proceedings of the 10th International Conference on Computational Creativity. Association for Computational Creativity, Charlotte, NC, USA, 17–21 June 2019; pp. 156–163. Available online: https://computationalcreativity.net/iccc2019/assets/iccc_proceedings_2019.pdf (accessed on 26 October 2020).
30. Veale, T.; Cardoso, F.A. *Computational Creativity: The Philosophy and Engineering of Autonomously Creative Systems*; Springer: Cham, Switzerland, 2019.
31. Ohsawa, Y. Modeling the process of chance discovery. In *Chance Discovery*; Springer: Cham, Switzerland, 2003; pp. 2–15.
32. Abe, A. Curation and communication in chance discovery. In Proceedings of the 6th International Workshop on Chance Discovery (IWCD6) in IJCAI, Barcelona, Spain, 6–18 July 2011.
33. Gadamer, H.G. *Literature and Philosophy in Dialogue: Essays in German Literary Theory*; SUNY Press: New York, NY, USA, 1994.

34. Hirsch, E.D. *Validity in Interpretation*; Yale University Press: Chelsea, MA, USA, 1967; Volume 260.
35. Fish, S.E. *Is There a Text in This Class?: The Authority of Interpretive Communities*; Harvard University Press: Cambridge, MA, USA, 1980.
36. Eco, U. Towards a semiotic inquiry into the television message. In *Working Papers in Cultural Studies*; Translated by Paola Splendore; Blackwell Publishing: London, UK, 1972; Volume 3, pp. 103–121.
37. Whitehead, J. *Madness and the Romantic Poet: A Critical History*; Oxford University Press: Oxford, UK, 2017.
38. Dennett, D.C. The self as the center of narrative gravity. In *Self and Consciousness*; Psychology Press: Hove, UK, 2014; pp. 111–123.
39. Radford, A.; Wu, J.; Child, R.; Luan, D.; Amodei, D.; Sutskever, I. Language models are unsupervised multitask learners. *OpenAI Blog* **2019**, *1*, 9.
40. Devlin, J.; Chang, M.W.; Lee, K.; Toutanova, K. BERT: Pre-training of Deep Bidirectional Transformers for Language Understanding. In Proceedings of the 2019 Conference of the North American Chapter of the Association for Computational Linguistics: Human Language Technologies, Volume 1 (Long and Short Papers), Minneapolis, MN, USA, 2–7 June 2019; pp. 4171–4186.
41. Graves, A. Generating sequences with recurrent neural networks. *arXiv* **2013**, arXiv:1308.0850.
42. Blanke, O.; Landis, T.; Spinelli, L.; Seeck, M. Out-of-body experience and autoscopy of neurological origin. *Brain* **2004**, *127*, 243–258. [CrossRef] [PubMed]
43. Tikhonov, A. *Paranoid Transformer*; NEW SIGHT: 2020. Available online: https://deadalivemagazine.com/press/paranoid-transformer.html (accessed on 26 October 2020).
44. Ha, D.; Eck, D. A neural representation of sketch drawings. *arXiv* **2017**, arXiv:1704.03477.
45. Bocharov, S.G. *O Hudozhestvennyh Mirah*. Moscow, Russia, 1985; pp. 161–209. Available online: https://imwerden.de/pdf/bocharov_o_khudozhestvennykh_mirakh_1985_text.pdf (accessed on 26 October 2012).
46. Dostoevsky, F. Zapiski iz podpolya - Notes from Underground. *Povesti i rasskazy v 2 t* **1984**, *2*, 287–386.
47. Turing, A.M. Computing machinery and intelligence. *Mind* **1950**, *59*, 433. [CrossRef]
48. Jamwal, V. Exploring the Notion of Self in Creative Self-Expression. In Proceedings of the 10th International Conference on Computational Creativity ICCC19, Charlotte, NC, USA, 17–21 June 2019; pp. 331–335.
49. Locke, J. *An Essay Concerning Human Understanding: And a Treatise on the Conduct of the Understanding*; Hayes & Zell: Philadelphia, PA, USA, 1860.
50. Perišić, M.M.; Štorga, M.; Gero, J. Situated novelty in computational creativity studies. In Proceedings of the 10th International Conference on Computational Creativity ICCC19, Charlotte, NC, USA, 17–21 June 2019; pp. 286–290.

MDPI
St. Alban-Anlage 66
4052 Basel
Switzerland
Tel. +41 61 683 77 34
Fax +41 61 302 89 18
www.mdpi.com

Future Internet Editorial Office
E-mail: futureinternet@mdpi.com
www.mdpi.com/journal/futureinternet

www.ingramcontent.com/pod-product-compliance
Lightning Source LLC
LaVergne TN
LVHW070043120526
838202LV00101B/415
* 9 7 8 3 0 3 6 5 3 7 4 0 5 *